Inventing Texas

NUMBER NINETY-SIX:

Centennial Series of the
Association of Former Students,
Texas A&M University

INVENTING
TEXAS

Early Historians

OF THE

Lone Star State

★ ★ ★ ★ ★ ★

LAURA LYONS MCLEMORE

Texas A&M University Press ★ College Station

The paper used in this book meets the minimum requirements
of the American National Standard for Permanence
of Paper for Printed Library Materials, z39.48-1984.
Binding materials have been chosen for durability.
∞

Library of Congress Cataloging-in-Publication Data
McLemore, Laura Lyons, 1950–
Inventing Texas : early historians of the Lone Star State / Laura
Lyons McLemore.—1st ed.
p. cm.—(Centennial series of the Association of Former
Students, Texas A&M University ; no. 96)
Includes bibliographical references (p.) and index.
ISBN 1-58544-314-X (cloth : alk. paper)
1. Texas—Historiography. 2. Texas—History—18th
century—Chronology. 3. Texas—History—19th century—Chronolgy. 4.
Folklore—Texas. 5. Historians—Texas—Biography. I. Title. II.
Series
F385.2 .M35 2004
976.4'007'202—dc22
2003016353

In memory of my father,
VAL ALEXANDER LYONS

Contents

Acknowledgments

Many individuals have contributed both directly and indirectly to the completion of this project. Randolph B. Campbell, my mentor and friend, deserves special thanks for listening, answering my questions, making suggestions, and offering encouragement from the conception of it to the conclusion. I also wish to thank Donald E. Chipman and James Ward Lee for their advice, encouragement, and support, and Walter L. Buenger for providing a critical reading of the original manuscript.

I am deeply indebted to archivists and librarians at the Center for American History at the University of Texas, Houston Public Library Metropolitan Research Center, and the Texas State Archives for their assistance in locating and making available original sources, and to interlibrary loan staff at the University of North Texas and Austin College, who frequently went out of their way to obtain hard-to-find publications for me.

The Center for American History at the University of Texas assisted my early research with the Miss Ima Hogg Research Travel Award, and the Texas State Historical Association gave financial support through the John H. Jenkins Research Fellowship.

Finally, I owe a huge debt of gratitude to my family for their patience and support, both moral and financial, throughout the long process of research and writing.

Inventing Texas

Introduction

Have you heard the one about the Yankee businessman who, familiar with all the stories about Texas, found himself one day in Fort Worth for a convention? He ordered a steak in the hotel restaurant and was astounded when it was served on a plate the size of a wagon wheel.

"Oh," explained the waiter, "you know everything's big in Texas."

The Yankee was even more amazed when the martini he ordered arrived in a glass the size of a five-gallon bucket.

"Oh," giggled the cocktail waitress, "you know everything's big in Texas."

Not surprisingly, the conventioneer soon found himself just a little woozy and in need of the facilities.

"Which way to the men's room?" he asked the waiter.

"It's through those double doors, sir, first door on the left," came the reply.

So off the foreigner wobbled to relieve himself. He passed through the double doors and found himself in a hallway with doors on the right and left. In his inebriated state, he could not recall the waiter's instructions. After a moment's hesitation, he pushed through the door on the right and within two steps stumbled with a mighty splash into the hotel swimming pool. In his panic, only one thought penetrated his consciousness.

"Don't flush!" he cried. "For God's sake, don't flush!"

This is, of course, a silly, cocktail party joke, but it illustrates a popular conception of the Lone Star State that Texans are inclined to exploit and that many are loathe to give up. Texas has a larger-than-life image that some late-twentieth-century historians of the state insist was invented by their counterparts in the nineteenth century, an image, they maintain, that inhibits the full development of Texas history and creates a sense of what it means to be Texan that "precludes many of the state's citizens from identifying themselves as Texans."[1] C. Vann Woodward estimated the shelf life of history—that is, the period between generational revisions of it—to be about twenty years.[2] The shelf life of Texas history, by contrast, seems to be approaching two hundred.

Walter Buenger and Robert Calvert, in the introduction to their 1991 collection of historiographical essays, *Texas through Time,* pointed out that the revising of old myths requires both an understanding of their origins and an understanding of how past generations looked at the past.[3] My purpose here is to take a brief look into the writing of the earliest historians on Texas in an effort to understand the origins of enduring Texas myths and the way the generations who have been credited with giving life to them looked at Texas history.

In my reading of early histories of Texas, several facts became readily apparent. I realized first that what we generally refer to as the Texas myth was reality to the would-be Texas historians of the eighteenth and nineteenth centuries and, second, that myth has always been an integral part of Texas history, providing the impetus for some of the earliest European interest in it. As Joe B. Frantz once pointed out, "Coronado did set out four hundred years ago, bedazzled by the storied wealth of a region somewhere in the direction of Texas; Texans did carve out an area the size of modern France or Germany and made an independent nation of it; Texans did suffer mightily at the Alamo and Goliad, regardless of how or why they got there; they did triumph at San Jacinto over a vastly superior army;" and, there is no getting around the fact that certain physical features of Texas can only be described in superlatives: features of climate, geography, and natural resources.[4] I also realized that those who wrote about Texas in preceding centuries were not simply spinning yarns. A survey of the work of Texas' nineteenth-century historians reveals that they were, by and large, painstaking and discriminating researchers whose legacy includes, in some cases, documentary sources that can no longer be found elsewhere. I noticed, too (and significantly, I think), that the vast majority wrote general works. Finally, I realized that the early writers of Texas history, with few exceptions, had agendas that frequently had little to do with simply explaining a society to itself in cultural terms.

All of these characteristics may be observed in the writing of Texas history beginning with Juan Agustín Morfi's *History* in the late eighteenth century and continuing into the twentieth century. The writing of Morfi, as well as that of José Antonio Pichardo, both products of the Spanish regime, was based on meticulous research. Both of these early historians made exhaustive and critical use of sources and strove for objectivity, but neither would have written at all had he not been prompted to do so by practical considerations: Morfi in response to attacks on Franciscan missionaries in Texas and Pichardo in response, essentially, to the Louisiana Purchase. Both produced documentary histories, yet neither was immune to myth and legend. Morfi described Texas as an earthly paradise—neither too hot nor too cold, seldom a cloudy sky, healthy and ageless inhabitants, abundant flora and fauna, fertile soil exceeding all exaggeration, and incredible numbers of wild horses and cattle.[5] Pichardo developed a thesis, backed by thorough research, that the province of Quivira visited by Coronado was on the plains of Cíbola and was actually the province of Texas.[6] The idea of Texas as a place apart thus found its way into the history books before the first Anglo-American settlers ever arrived.

By the end of the first quarter of the nineteenth century, the American Romantic Movement was under way, and it was to have a profound and lasting effect on the way Americans viewed the world and their place in it. Moreover, history was considered literature, and writers of the 1830s and 1840s conformed to the model of novelists like Sir Walter Scott. Historians of the Spanish borderlands had before them the works of Washington Irving and William H. Prescott to emulate. History, filled as it was with battles, heroes and villains, and adventures in the wilderness, was romantic by its very nature and a tremendously popular subject with the reading public. This fact did not escape those writing histories of Texas. Texas was "a happening place," so to speak, and it drew both curiosity seekers and fortune seekers in the years between the first Anglo-American settlement and its annexation to the United States. Those who wrote Texas history during the second quarter of the nineteenth century did so for a variety of reasons, most related in one way or another to personal interests. Mary Austin Holley, for example, wrote to assist her cousin Stephen F. Austin in his enterprise. After all, she had a stake in increasing land values in the colony, but she was also one of those female "scribblers," as the famous American writer Nathaniel Hawthorne called them, who wrote to support herself and her children. By her own admission, she perceived that Texas was a topic likely to sell books. And she was right. Her first book, *Texas: Observations Historical, Geographical, and Descriptive* (1833), would have had to sell at least five hundred copies to net her after-tax estimated profit of four hundred to five hundred dollars. Her 1836 *Texas* reputedly sold double that number, or about a thousand copies. Other historians, such as David B. Edward (*The History of Texas*, 1836) and N. Doran Maillard (*History of the Republic of Texas*, 1842), both blatantly anti-Texan, had a stake in Mexican interests in the province. European visitors, such as Frédéric LeClerc (*Texas and Its Revolution*, 1840) and William Kennedy (*Texas: The Rise, Progress, and Prospects of the Republic of Texas*, 1841), were genuinely curious, but then, both France and England had economic and political reasons for being interested in Texas. And one cannot deny that the revolutionary phenomenon contributed to European fascination with Texas. "I could not clearly understand," wrote William Kennedy, "how the settlers of Texas were enabled to repel the armies of Mexico and to found a Republic of their own."[7]

The reality that escaped neither LeClerc nor Kennedy was that these Americans had been able to repeat this feat no less than three times in fifty years, not only against the larger force of Mexico but twice against England, the mightiest nation on earth.

Unquestionably, these writers made use of available sources. Edward, though guilty of plagiarizing Holley, included in his book full texts of pertinent Mexican laws and the full text of the proposed Constitution of 1833, an appendix containing census statistics, and a translation of the Mexican Constitution of 1824. Kennedy's sources were the most thorough to date, as he had access to the remarkable collection of Mirabeau Lamar.

Others whose curiosity brought them to Texas, such as missionaries Chester Newell (*History of Texas and Its Revolution,* 1838) and A. B. Lawrence (*Texas in 1840* and *History of Texas,* 1844), and Edward Stiff (*The Texan Emigrant,* 1840), who simply had an eye out for the main chance wherever he might find it, turned to history writing to defray the expenses of their trips and, perhaps as a bonus in the case of the missionaries, to engage in a bit of moral instruction. Henry S. Foote (*Texas and the Texans,* 1841) had as straightforward a reason for writing a romantic, pro-Texan history as there could be. He was hired to do so by Mirabeau Lamar, then president of the Republic of Texas. If these writers were given to hyperbole, drama, and hero making, they were the products of their times. Nevertheless, with rare exception, they conscientiously sought and relied on primary sources as well as personal observation, and most were methodical and critical in their use of them. All ardently proclaimed their impartiality and objectivity, though all were just as ardently biased in favor of either Texas or Mexico. Some made heroes of Sam Houston and the Alamo defenders, while others cast aspersions on the character of Texans in general and the revolutionists in particular. Taken as a whole, they provided a fairly balanced analysis of Texas history through the war of independence from Mexico.

By the 1850s, changes began to take place in the approach to history writing generally. Some of these changes appeared in Texas history. José Antonio Navarro and William Gouge, for example, departed from the practice of writing general histories and focused on more limited topics: in Navarro's case, a series of articles on the historical contributions of Tejanos, and in Gouge's, *A Fiscal History of Texas* (1852). The study of history was gradually coming to be regarded as something more than a branch of literature. In keeping with the shift in approach from general to particular, state histories were becoming popular. Ten years after the official dissolution of the republic, Texans were still awaiting the definitive history of their state. Henderson Yoakum, an attorney from Huntsville and close associate of Sam Houston, remedied the situation with his two-volume *History of Texas* in 1855. Yoakum's *History,* the most thoroughly researched and documented to date, became the benchmark well into the twentieth century, a fact that was fraught with implications for "the shelf life" of Texas history.

Yoakum's work, from the time of its publication, was one of the most highly regarded of all the state histories written during the antebellum era. It was also very much a product of its times: laboriously researched and documented, and thoroughly romantic. Yoakum altered direct quotes "to improve the accuracy of impression" when he believed his alterations came closer to the speaker's true intention (as he determined that to be). He portrayed the period prior to Anglo-American settlement as the dark ages of Texas history, the Anglo-Americans as freedom fighters, and Mexicans as evil despots.[8]

Yoakum's history was touted for its objectivity, yet he had no less an agenda than did his predecessors. Yoakum was a staunch Jacksonian, dedicated to agrarian republicanism and imperial expansion of the Union. When his political career in Tennessee and his ideology were threatened by Whig reforms in the early 1840s, he settled on Texas as the place to reconstruct his dream of an ideal republic. In 1845, he wrote to Martin Van Buren that the western land belonged to the American agrarian because God planned for democrats like himself to displace the "savage" and enrich the land.[9] In 1855, he used the vehicle of his history of Texas to promote this idea.

Ironically, contemporary reaction was far more critical than that of later generations. In 1855, reviewers criticized Yoakum's inability to escape his "biases and sympathies" for his bosom friend Sam Houston "so as to give an impartial and unprejudiced narrative."[10] But by 1898, one compiler stated that he could not improve upon it substantially enough to supersede it, and another historiographer called Yoakum's work "the accepted standard of authority." In 1935, "it was consulted by writers of history the world over and regarded as the standard for the period it covers." In 1945, another editor asserted that it "achieved an unusual degree of objectivity," and Eugene C. Barker, then dean of Texas historians, considered it the first history of Texas to meet the standards of professional historians.[11] Thus, by the mid-twentieth century, it was more highly regarded than it had been by nineteenth-century contemporaries.

Histories of Texas written in the decade following the Civil War reflected the effects of that bitter episode on the collective psyche of the state. Suffering from the humiliation of being on the losing side and the perception that they had been deprived of their self-determination by Reconstruction, Texans embraced the idea of rescuing their own heroes from oblivion and experienced a burst of renewed Texas nationalism. Among the first products of this renewed interest in the revolutionary generation and the memorialization of heroes were the works of DeWitt Clinton Baker and James Morphis.

Both Morphis and Baker wrote what British historian R. G. Collingwood referred to as the "scissors and paste" method of history, that is, a patchwork drawn from the works of previous historians.[12] Morphis's work (*History of Texas From Its Discovery and Settlement,* 1874) was a rehash of the work of Kennedy and Yoakum, combining whole texts of original documents and creative narrative. Morphis devoted the bulk of his work to the Texas Revolution, allowing two and a half pages for the period from 1685 to 1823 and only a dozen or so to the Civil War. He ended with an example of a Texas tall tale and a poetic benediction to Progress. The New York *Turf, Field, and Farm* called it an "exceedingly clever production," and the *Dallas Weekly Herald* praised it for its "humorous anecdotes," "droll" narration, and "pen pictures." The editors noted that the book also contained valuable information and historical data for those wishing "to read up on Texas."[13]

Prior to the appearance of Morphis's book, Baker published a Texas history textbook in 1873 that was condemned by Redeemer Texans for expressing anti-Southern views. Baker's purpose was twofold: to promote state history in public schools and to make money. When the first book failed to sell, he produced his better-known *Texas Scrapbook* (1875), a compilation designed for the casual reader. The volume included anecdotes, poems, speeches, statistics, and biographical sketches of war dead, San Jacinto veterans, and other figures in Texas history. It offered something for everyone: uninterpreted facts, colorful narrative, even sentimental poetry. It was representative in its own time of Texans' concept of history, characterized by the desire to glorify the past and capture the nostalgia of pioneer life, which many feared was disappearing. Progress in the late nineteenth century threatened the ideal of an agrarian republic.[14] When Homer Thrall, Methodist preacher turned teacher, undertook a textbook (*History of Texas,* 1876) and later, *A Pictorial History of Texas* (1879), he, too, concentrated on the Texas Revolution and promoted Texas as the promised land. His attempts to treat sensitive subjects, such as slavery, neutrally and heroes objectively aroused intense ire among many Texans.

There were others who attempted, with limited success, to counter this nostalgic trend. Simultaneously with the upsurge of nostalgia during the Gilded Age, not just in Texas but all over the nation, the field of history writing was undergoing a paradigm shift. History had arrived in the university. Scientific history required more than a critical approach to evidence; among other things it involved the relation of things to one another. Reuben Potter and Hubert Howe Bancroft both approached Texas history in this way, Potter through a series of articles in Eastern papers and periodicals such as the *Magazine of American History* in the 1870s. He had witnessed the Texas Revolution and wrote primarily to correct the record. Potter dealt with subjects little touched upon since Yoakum, such as Tejanos and slavery. Both he and Bancroft perceived Texas history in terms of its impact on the larger context of the United States and the world. Neither gained much popularity with Texans.

Whereas Potter published articles on limited topics, Bancroft produced a new comprehensive study of Texas history. Bancroft went about his endeavor as scientifically and systematically as any professional. His goal, ultimately, was to be recognized as a scholar and to be respected among the learned elite. He spent a personal fortune amassing sources and hired a staff of researchers and writers to assist him in his project, not unlike professional historians at Eastern universities like Harvard, who were assisted by countless graduate students. Nevertheless, he was criticized harshly, and his editorial achievement was belittled by these same professional historians. His two volumes, *History of the North Mexican States and Texas, 1531–1889,* appeared in 1883 and 1889. They were enormously important to Texas history but little appreciated by his contemporaries. Bancroft and Potter were in many ways casualties of growing elitism in the historical profession and the growing nostalgia of the post-Reconstruction South. Bancroft's volumes were dismissed by professional historians as local history; Potter became better known for his sentimental poem "Hymn of the Alamo," written in 1836, than for his later articles on the Texas Revolution and republic.

Texas history in the last decade of the nineteenth century was the subject of a number of cooperative "memorial" or "vanity" histories, all of them by amateurs, among them Dudley G. Wooten and John Henry Brown. Wooten's endeavor combined adherence to romantic principles and nostalgia with the more recent scientific method in the gathering of specialized monographs. The result was a Texas souvenir as much as anything, and, typically, it was big (two oversized volumes and nearly two thousand pages). C. W. Raines summed it up in a wonderfully ironic masterpiece of understatement: "This work is something more than a history in the ordinary acceptance of the term."[15]

Brown, veteran of the Texas Revolution, the Texas Rangers, the Mexican War, and the Civil War, attempted to expand his memoirs into a comprehensive history of Texas (*History of Texas from 1685 to 1892,* 1892–93). He spent fifty years collecting material for his history and four years writing it. In the end, it was a memorial to himself and the republican agrarian ideal. One reviewer observed that Brown's work could "be scrutinized in vain to find a deliberate utterance antagonistic to public or private virtue or unfaithful to the glory of Texas."[16]

Nevertheless, by the last decades of the nineteenth century, professional history seemed to be gaining ground with the establishment of the Department of History at the University of Texas. George P. Garrison, chair of the newly created department in 1889, was a Georgia native who received his training as a historian at the University of Chicago. Like Bancroft, Garrison saw Texas history as an aspect of United States history. He inspired Texas historians to interpret and write about Texas not only as part of the westward movement of the United States but as part of a larger manifest destiny. One of his students, Lester Gladstone Bugbee, provided the bridge between Garrison's nationalistic emphasis and regional approaches to Texas history beginning with the Southwestern emphasis.

In addition, Garrison realized that professional methods of research, to be of value, ultimately had to be transmuted into common knowledge. In an effort to accomplish this, with the help of Lester Bugbee and others he established the Texas State Historical Association in 1897 and invited the state's history-minded citizens and high-ranking politicians to join. Soon the pages of the association's *Quarterly* were filled with the reminiscences and nostalgia of countless amateur historians whom Garrison, as editor, instructed in scientific methods as he published their work.

Obviously, then, although early Texas historians may have possessed a variety of agendas and a romantic style more literary than analytical, those whose work survives seem to have been mostly conscientious in their research and at least aware of the need for objectivity. Change did occur in the writing of Texas history as in American historiography, generally, and by the end of the nineteenth century, professional historians were turning their attention to it. What then prompts writer Larry McMurtry and others to question whether Texas has ever had an unsentimental historian? "Escaping the enfolding snares of past writings requires understanding their origins," write Buenger and Calvert. Thus, a closer examination of Texas' nineteenth-century historians seems long overdue.[17]

1 ★ Prologue

Historians of Spanish Texas

As many historians have pointed out, in order to gain insight into the writing of history in any age, one must have some knowledge of the climate of opinion at that time, some understanding of the historical paradigm that influenced the historian. The idea that history should serve some useful purpose predated the nineteenth century. It derived from the philosophy of the Enlightenment in the late eighteenth century, which affected both the style and content of historical writing in Europe and America and, ultimately, in Spanish America. Inevitably, it influenced the writing of Texas history in the nineteenth century as surely as the events of the late eighteenth century affected the unfolding of Texas history in the nineteenth century. When the first formal history of the province as a distinct geographical entity was drafted near the end of the eighteenth century, it had as its inspiration a calculated purpose. The persuasive paradigm, the "myth with a message," actually originated with the historians of Spanish Texas. They wrote the prologue for nineteenth-century Texas history.

On the eve of the nineteenth century, an industrious, devoted, and learned Franciscan missionary, Fray Juan Agustín Morfi, wrote the first comprehensive history of the far northern province of New Spain known as Tejas, which he described as lying 360 leagues from the city of Mexico, bounded by the Gulf of Mexico and Nuevo Santander (Tamaulipas) on the south, Nuevo Reyno de León and the province of Coahuila on the west, by New Mexico on the north and northwest, and by the English colonies and Louisiana on the east.[1] Morfi did not set out to become a historian, much less a Texas historian. In fact, he did not even set out to become a priest. Born in the Spanish province of Asturias, he probably came to America in 1755 or 1756. According to records in Mexico, he came as a layman and joined the Franciscan order in Mexico City on May 3, 1761. Thus, he appears to have come, as did so many others, in search of fame and fortune. Morfi taught theology in the old college of Santa Cruz de Tlatelolco under the direction of the Franciscans and wrote treatises on the subject.[2] In a short time he made quite a reputation for himself as an orator and lecturer.

Morfi developed his deep interest in Texas and the work of missionaries there during his coerced performance as chaplain to Teodoro de Croix on his tour of inspection in 1777. Initially, Morfi assumed the role of collector and compiler. He kept a careful diary that included information he was able to glean from local archives wherever the expedition stopped. After his return from that trip, he began actively to collect all the documents he could find on the provinces he had visited. Over the short space of five years, from 1778 to 1783, Morfi labored tirelessly to assemble the sources for the history of all northern Mexico—more than eight thousand pages on Texas alone—in order to complete the information in the Franciscan archives.[3] He made the transition from compiler to historian when his work took on a more specific purpose.

Morfi's impetus came from Antonio Bonilla's *Breve Compendio de la Historia de Texas* (1772), which blamed the missionaries for the failure of the various attempts to colonize Texas.[4] Deeply offended by this imputation, Morfi turned to the writing of a history in defense of his Franciscan brethren, who, his travels with Teodoro de Croix had convinced him, were heroic and unselfish. He intended to vindicate them by presenting the facts. He had already compiled his sources and organized them roughly in his *Memorias para la Historia de Texas* with the express purpose of proving that incompetent officials and flawed government policy, not the missionaries, were to blame for Spain's failures in Texas.[5] From his *Memorias,* Morfi commenced to write his *Historia de Texas,* which was later translated and published as the *History of Texas, 1673–1779.*

Although he adhered generally to a strict chronological arrangement, Morfi began his *History* with a detailed description of the province of Texas, its location and boundaries, its rivers and creeks, settlements, and native tribes, based on the most authoritative accounts known. Though this detail might well have been reflective of the prevailing Enlightenment interest in natural history, the land he described might easily have been imagined an earthly paradise by his readers: neither too hot nor too cold, seldom a cloudy sky, enough rain but not too much, mild winters, storms and earthquakes unheard of, healthy and ageless inhabitants, abundant flora and fauna, fertile soil "exceeding all exaggeration," and incredible numbers of wild horses and cattle.[6] This perception of Texas as a New World Eden would provide a link between the Spanish and the eager inheritors of the Puritan mission into the wilderness who flocked to Texas in the nineteenth century.[7]

Morfi demonstrated further his determination to be matter-of-fact in his description of the native inhabitants. On the basis of the reports of missionaries and Spanish officials, he characterized the inhabitants of the province neither as noble savages nor as inferior races but simply as heathens in need of redemption, possessing both strengths and weaknesses. He admitted that many of these peoples either would not or could not adapt to mission life and teachings. He also noted, regretfully, that the character and the lives of some of them had been irreparably disrupted and altered through their arbitrary relocation by Spanish stratagems.[8] However difficult or unsuited some or even a majority of the natives might be for missionization, he concluded that the missions offered Spain's best hope of maintaining control of Texas.

Morfi began his chronological account with Hernando De Soto's expedition in 1543 and ended abruptly with the death of Athanese De Mézières (because Morfi himself died in October 1783). Whenever he departed from strict chronology, he took pains to explain and justify the digression. He apparently considered his account of the French expeditions, René-Robert Cavalier Sieur de La Salle's attempt to settle on Matagorda Bay and the appearance of Louis Juchereau de St. Denis at the presidio of San Juan Bautista, a long digression, because he explained the necessity of it by writing that the events of the history of Louisiana were so closely connected with those of Texas that he found it impossible to describe what took place in the latter without giving a summary of the former.[9] In so doing, he acknowledged the connectedness of historical events, the acts of individuals, and the notion of cause and effect.

Throughout his manuscript, Morfi numbered the paragraphs and included marginal topical headings to guide the reader. He obviously attempted to give a cohesive narrative, but just as clearly his purpose was to prove, by presenting the facts, the injustice that had been done to the missionaries in Texas by Bonilla's report. Certainly, Morfi accumulated and presented a wealth of information from the most reliable sources available, but he also unmistakably interpreted them from his own bias as he paused to point out with bitter passion the weaknesses in the reforms of Field Marshall Don Pedro de Rivera in 1728, the evils resulting from his policies, and the failure of the Texas missions because of changing policies of Spanish officials and the jealousy and ambition of presidial captains.[10] Through it all, Morfi succeeded in presenting fairly and convincingly the evidence of the heroic efforts of the Franciscans to Christianize the natives. The success of his rational and objective achievement was measured both by his contemporaries and by later historians. Fray José Antonio Pichardo quoted from Morfi's *History* in discussing English traders in Texas, the activities of St. Denis, La Salle's expedition and settlement, Peñalosa in New Mexico and in the French court, Ibarbo's exploration of the Gulf coast, the death of La Salle, French Indian traders, Blancpain's activities, and the history of New Mexico. Hubert Howe Bancroft late in the nineteenth century called it "the standard authority for Texas history" up to the date of Morfi's death.[11]

At the time of his death in 1783, Morfi's *History* was unfinished, but his legacy to future Texas historians was established. He was thorough in his collection of sources and was critical in his treatment of them and direct in his presentation. By setting out to prove a thesis through the presentation and analysis of facts in a concise style, Morfi produced a thoroughly rational, secular history. Thus, the *History* provided the standard to which the next major Texas historian, and first of the nineteenth century, turned for authority.[12]

The first general work on the history of Texas written in the nineteenth century did not appear until nearly thirty years later, in 1812, which was unsurprising in that Spain exhibited little interest in Texas until the Louisiana Purchase in 1803. That event irrevocably linked Texas' history with that of the United States from the very beginning of the nineteenth century and provided the purpose for another history. Further, Thomas Jefferson's subsequent assertions that the boundary of the Louisiana Purchase extended to the Rio Grande, together with the intrusions of American filibusters like Philip Nolan, made the need for a history of the Spanish presence in Texas more urgent.[13] This history, a treatise on the boundary between Louisiana and Texas, was also the work of an enlightened ecclesiastic, José Antonio Pichardo of the archbishopric of Mexico. Pichardo was a *criollo* (Mexican-born Spaniard) born in Cuernavaca, Mexico, in 1748 and educated at the very old college of San Juan de Letrán, where he became a professor of Latin and philosophy.[14] That he should be thoroughly versed in Enlightenment thought seems doubtless for several reasons. Through the work of Arthur P. Whitaker, John Tate Lanning, and other scholars, we know that modern philosophy and science were known and expounded in the eighteenth-century schools and universities of the Spanish colonies in America. Pichardo enjoyed the reputation of being one of the most educated men in Mexico. He amassed a personal library of some six thousand volumes and was purported to have read and used them all. He knew, in addition to Greek and Latin, the principal modern languages, as evidenced by frequent references in his works to French, Italian, English, and Dutch authorities. Further, his predecessor in the writing of the history of the boundary between Texas and Louisiana, Fray Melchor de Talamantes, was a brilliant scholar and political liberal removed from his assignment for his revolutionary leanings, a matter of which Pichardo must have been aware.[15]

Pichardo undertook the research and writing of Talamantes's monumental project in 1808. From the outset, his work shared a number of characteristics with that of Morfi, whose *Notes* and *History* he cited as sources. Both authors used a format of numbered paragraphs, though Pichardo, in addition, divided his work into an introduction and four parts. Like Morfi, Pichardo based his work on a thesis. Unlike Morfi, however, Pichardo did not attempt a strict narrative history; his method was wholly argumentative, his authorities and sources carefully selected to prove his points.[16] He did not stint on scientific measurements and mathematical proof with regard to his geographical assertions. He plainly intended to be thoroughly scientific in the belief that this method would ensure his objectivity and render his conclusions unquestionable. "I have endeavored always to give proofs of what I am saying," he wrote, "and . . . I refer to what I have already proven, or what I must prove in due time, or I cite near the writing the texts of the authors or documents upon which I have based my assertion. My work has been long drawn out, but I have preferred to lay myself liable to this offense to that of making myself obscure because of brevity, and unworthy of credit because of the weakness of my sources."[17]

Pichardo quoted extensively from his sources. His own comments seem to have been inserted mainly to state his argument, to introduce a quotation, and to point out how it proved his thesis. He included virtually no important event connected with his subject without referring to basic primary sources relating to it, and he made use of secondary printed works, more than one hundred books, pamphlets, and maps written or printed prior to 1811.[18] Unlike those Enlightenment historians who achieved fame by literary style, epigram, and wit, Pichardo was not concerned with literary device but with clarity. He believed that, properly stated, the facts would speak for themselves.

For all his meticulous and painstaking efforts at objectivity, Pichardo could not escape the subjectivity inherent in advocacy. Considering the circumstances that prompted his writing of the boundary history—that is, royal orders of the viceroy of Mexico—he could hardly have been otherwise. He made many honest concessions to practical realities, such as the admission that "despite the injustice with which the French appropriated for themselves all the land of Louisiana," La Salle's claim, however ignorant or erroneous it may have been on his part, justified the belief of the French at Natchitoches in 1735 that their territory extended to Arroyo Hondo. However, Pichardo never conceded that the French had a legitimate right to any of the Louisiana territory. Instead, he maintained, the Spanish monarch simply allowed them this delusion out of the goodness of his heart and nobility of spirit in order to "avoid wars and the effusion of human blood."[19] He admitted that the boundary question had not been disputed when France ceded its claim to Spain in 1762, because neither party really cared much about Texas, absent any third-party interest. With sharp foresight, Pichardo recognized that the acute interest of the United States in the region prompted "the necessity for a concise history of the boundary question." However, he hastened to portray Spain's intentions as purely noble and fiscally responsible: "She is so upright and so faithful in the performance of duty that, once made the compact of retrocession, she does not wish to retain any of that which she received and has ceded. But she is at the same time so frugal that she does not wish to squander that which she has not included in her compacts."[20]

In furtherance of his historical argument, Pichardo began with the discovery of America and the papal grant. He discussed the French expeditions of Giovanni da Verrazano and Jacques Cartier to the Atlantic coast and recognized the first presence of the French in the Louisiana territory in the persons of Jacques Marquette and Louis Jolliet in 1673. He dated the history of Texas as a distinct province from the settlement of El Paso in 1693. In the opinion of historian Charles W. Hackett, editor and translator of the *Treatise,* Pichardo's greatest contribution to the historical record was the detailing of significant and little-known events that occurred in the Spanish province of Texas during the last three-quarters of the eighteenth century. But Pichardo reached perhaps his most intriguing conclusion with his physical description of Texas in which he developed the thesis that the province of Quivira, which Francisco Vásquez de Coronado visited, was on the plains of Cíbola and was actually the province of Texas.[21] However faulty this conclusion, he found a way to support it scientifically, based on thorough and accurate study of the available sources, his own profound knowledge of the Indian tribes of the plains of Cíbola, geography of the region, comparison of Indian names given by early writers, the application of mathematics, and other critical methods of comparison and research.[22] In doing so, he demonstrated the same tendency of both his Spanish predecessors and his American successors to use scientific history to perpetuate a Texas myth—part mission, part destiny, part redemptive bounty of a New World Eden.

So began the writing of Texas history in the nineteenth century, with two highly educated, enlightened ecclesiastics devoted to a scientific method of arriving at the truths they knew and strongly influenced by their respective arguments. Morfi, though writing in the late eighteenth century, set a precedent for the writing of Texas history that set it apart from earlier histories of New Spain. The writing of both these men reflected the intellectual and political climate of their times. As members of the ordered Catholic clergy and as Spanish subjects, their viewpoints were somewhat limited by loyalty to their mission brethren (in Morfi's case) or loyalty to the Spanish crown (in Pichardo's case). Nevertheless, their work exhibited a self-conscious effort at objectivity, a search for cause-and-effect relationships in the actions of humans and the evidence of physical science rather than in miracles and the capriciousness of a willful God, an inductive method, abundant sources, and a critical, direct style. Yet, their style and content did not prevent them from perpetuating or attempting to corroborate certain aspects of New World mythology that extended to the frontier of Texas. It remained there to be shared with future generations of Texans and Texas historians. Professor Frederico Onís, writing in the mid-twentieth century, emphasized the important role played by the United States in the spiritual transformation of Spanish America in the eighteenth century. "The intellectual relations between the Americas are not an invention of our day, as many believe," he wrote.[23] As both Morfi and Pichardo acknowledged, the American presence was a factor in writing about Texas. It would only become stronger. The next writer with a use of Texas history would be an American.

2 ⋆ Texas Historians *and the* Romantic Revolution

Americans, like Spaniards, had from the beginning many romantic elements in their view of the New World. By the end of the first quarter of the nineteenth century, the American Romantic Movement was under way, and it was to have a profound and lasting effect on the way Americans viewed the world and their place in it. Whereas the Enlightenment emphasis on science and reason influenced the writing of the earliest Texas historians, romanticism produced greater emphasis on cultural evolution, mysticism, and universal themes. Moreover, to the writers of the romantic era, literary style assumed greater importance. History was considered literature, and writers of the 1830s and 1840s conformed to the model of novelists like Sir Walter Scott and James Fenimore Cooper. Historians of the Spanish borderlands had before them the works of Washington Irving and William Hickling Prescott to emulate. History, filled as it was with battles, heroes and villains, and adventures in the wilderness, was romantic by its very nature and a tremendously popular subject with the reading public, a fact that did not escape those writing histories of Texas.

The romantic era in America coincided with an explosion of growth in the book trade. Some consider it the golden age of literary production in the United States. Book production, in dollar terms, rose from an estimated $2.5 million in 1820 to $12.5 million in 1850, figures that confirm a great increase in reading between 1830 and 1840, attributable to new interest in primary and secondary education and the establishment of the penny press as well as many major periodicals.[1] The sheer number of Texas histories that appeared between 1819 and 1849 distinguished Texas history writing from that of other parts of the North American frontier. The bibliographies of early imprints related to Texas attest to the tremendous volume of publication.[2] During this period more than thirty monographs were published on Texas, at least a dozen of which claimed to be histories. Americans produced half of these; Europeans, the other half. All were visitors in Texas; none became permanent residents. They wrote about Texas history for a variety of reasons, mostly related in one way or another to personal interests. Certainly, they all expected to take advantage of the public's burgeoning appetite for books to make a profit.

Texas in the early nineteenth century became a hot political topic.[3] History, because it commanded a wide readership, became a favored medium for those deeply interested in the Texas controversy for personal or political reasons, who wished to appeal to public sentiment. Thus, though Texas historians might philosophize to some extent, they wrote primarily for more practical purposes. Unlike William Prescott, who created vividly accurate descriptions of Mexico and Peru from his sources without ever visiting either, none wrote about Texas without having experienced it firsthand, however brief the encounter. Almost without exception they had specific, pragmatic reasons for writing that rarely involved such lofty aims as teaching moral lessons, providing models for society, or demonstrating ultimate reality—the typical uses for romantic history. As a consequence, form followed function. They produced history as immigrant guide, polemic, legal brief, or stirring narrative as suited their specific purposes. Few wrote about Texas purely out of curiosity.

Europeans had been curious off and on for centuries. Perhaps even more compelling to European writers than the land itself was the phenomenon of the American revolutionary experience and America's peculiar brand of liberty, which spread rapidly as the century advanced. It provided a topic of immediate interest to their readers. American writers seemed, in this as in virtually every other field of American endeavor, compelled by a desire for gain of one sort or another.[4]

Americans demonstrated little preoccupation with Texas at the turn of the eighteenth century, but their attention to it increased considerably with the Louisiana Purchase and intensified with the struggles for Mexican and South American independence. Zebulon Pike's narrative, first published in 1810, spawned serious American interest in Texas. Even as early as Pike's account, American nativist attitudes appeared in print and were incorporated into perceptions of Texas.[5] That interest increased further with the signing of the Adams-Onís Treaty in 1819, an event that, combined with American fervor for the cause of liberty, prompted geographer and journalist William Darby to visit the vicinity and publish a short history of the ill-fated Gutiérrez-Magee expedition to Texas in 1813. "The existing state of our relations with Spain; the revolutionary state of the Spanish colonies in both the Americas: the part which many of our citizens have taken in that struggle; and finally, the policy which our government has and may continue to pursue, all tend to render interesting every subject connected with the Spanish colonies, particularly those in North America," he wrote.[6] Historians of American publishing confirm this claim. Frank L. Mott (*A History of American Magazines*) observed that after the Spanish Treaty of 1819, Cuban and Mexican relations were among the leading political topics in contemporary periodicals.[7]

Darby, who had grown up in the Ohio country, became a deputy United States surveyor after a fire destroyed his cotton plantation near Natchez, Mississippi, in 1804. Philadelphia publisher John Melish used his *Geographical Description of the State of Louisiana . . . Being an Accompaniment to the Map of Louisiana* (1816; 2d edition, 1817) as the basis for the boundary delineation in the treaty of 1819 between the United States and Spain. Unlike many subsequent nineteenth-century Texas historians, he wrote several books between 1817 and 1829 on the geography and history of the United States and North America that distinguished him professionally.[8]

Darby wrote his account of the province of Texas shortly after the battle for San Antonio but did not seek to publish it until "recent movements in Texas [gave] this sketch some interest." His article appeared in the *New York Columbian* on August 3, 1819, and in the highly respected *Niles Weekly Register* a few days later on August 7. *Niles* had a reputation for printing chiefly facts, statistics, speeches, and documents covering both sides of political and economic issues of the day. It was influential in its day and has remained a prime source for historians up to the present.[9] Darby's assessment was dispassionate, informed, and matter-of-fact, based on his personal observations as both a scientist and a journalist. His historic interpretation of the episode placed it in the context of world events and universal history. "It is not unworthy of remark," he observed, "that this petty war has been rendered memorable by the greatest extremes our nature is capable of." Darby condemned not only what he saw as the selfish and ignoble motives responsible for this episode but the unwillingness of Americans to educate themselves about the culture and perspective of the Spanish-Mexican population with whom they shared the continent. "If to engender confidence, friendship, and reciprocal forbearance, be an indispensable duty, in those who regulate the conduct, or who form the morals of private persons, how much more incumbent is the obligation on the rulers of nations, to preserve and foster a spirit of amity, probity, and urbanity, between contiguous states." The sad history of the Gutiérrez-Magee campaign proved, Darby argued, that filibusters, such as he judged this expedition to be, "prevent or retard the peaceable approach towards a general intercourse."[10]

When an American, Stephen F. Austin, established a colony in Texas and began to solicit emigrants from the United States, the fascination of the historian and the reading public with the mysterious and new fixed more fully on the province. This fascination, combined with a number of other, more mundane factors, produced what many generally regard as the first Anglo-American history of Texas and Texas' first historian, Mary Austin Holley.[11] Following her lead, writers of histories of Texas during the 1830s concentrated on the Anglo-European settlement of this vast region and its forcible separation from Mexico.

Holley, a cousin of the empresario Stephen F. Austin, not only exemplified many of the characteristics of the American romantic historians of the early nineteenth century but also set the example for early histories of Texas to follow in the years of the Texas Revolution and republic. Like many of the patrician historians, Holley, nee Austin, was born of a well-to-do New England family, moved in upper social circles, and received a fine education. Her father, Elijah Austin, was the older brother of Moses Austin. She married a Yale graduate, Horace Holley, a young clergyman who converted to Unitarianism and eventually became president of Transylvania University in Lexington, Kentucky. Reverend Holley had established himself in publishing circles as a respected and popular contributor to William Gibbes Hunt's *Western Review and Miscellaneous Magazine.* During her marriage to him, Mary Austin Holley moved in circles that included the Adamses, historian William Hickling Prescott, orator Edward Everett, and Henry Clay. Nevertheless, she turned to writing more out of financial necessity, prompted by the death of her husband in 1827, than out of inspiration.[12] Horace Holley's death left his wife in difficult circumstances with a mentally incompetent child to support. The loss prompted her first book, *A Discourse on the Genius and Character of the Rev. Horace Holley, LL. D.,* a defense of her husband's record at Transylvania University that was surprisingly well received and established for her something of a literary reputation. She became one of a growing number of women in America at the time who turned to writing to support themselves and their families.

Her second motive for writing about Texas was also financial, for she had been persuaded by her brother and cousins to become a land speculator and hence acquired a vested interest in promoting Texas. She never settled permanently there, but her brief visit in the fall of 1831 to claim her league of Texas land produced two enduring works of Texas literature: *Texas: Observations Historical, Geographical and Descriptive,* a collection of letters published in 1833, which made no pretense of being anything other than promotional; and *Texas,* published in 1836, which started out that way. *Texas* was to have been based largely on the first volume, topically organized with chapters on geography, rivers, soil and climate, trade, society and manners, money, banks, and mail, "strictly a matter of fact volume."[13] But even as she wrote, the events in Texas turned toward revolution and prompted her to change her emphasis. Texas needed more than vigorous immigration; it needed political support, and Holley determined to use her writing and extensive connections to further the Texas cause in the United States. As a result of her efforts to include each historic event as it occurred, she produced a hastily assembled account of the Texas Revolution and birth of the new republic, entitled simply *Texas*. Ironically, the first book brought her the greatest critical acclaim and was influential enough that David B. Edward and other historians of the era plagiarized it. Plainly, however, Mary Holley herself considered the second book to be the more important of the two and to be the basis of her claim to the designation "historian."[14]

In fact, though it began as a travelogue and immigrant guide, Holley's *Texas* bore many of the characteristics of the romantic history being written in America at the time, such as the personification of nature. The description of geography, climate, soil, streams, and native races with which the volume opened, in addition to providing general information to the prospective immigrant, satisfied the contemporary requirement that modern history, as a science, endeavor to understand "the real geography of a country, its organic structure; the form of its skeleton, that is, of its hills; the magnitude and course of its veins and arteries, that is, of its streams and rivers; to conceive of it as a whole, made up of connected parts . . . exhibiting these two elements—the geographico-climatic and the human—in their mutual action and reaction."[15] Nor did she neglect to identify cause and effect in the unfolding of events. Holley's style, replete with classical references and nature metaphors, reflected the demand that history be picturesque as well as accurate. The pages of her history abounded in classical references and the obligatory romantic heroes and villains, elevated the common man, and idealized frontier agrarianism: "The blood-hounds of Mexico" tore up "every vestage [*sic*] of civilization." Texas "had her *Leonidas,* and many a *Curtius,*" and every man would "become a *Cincinnatus.*"[16]

As easily identifiable as elements of romantic style were the prevalent themes of American romantic history in Holley's *Texas:* morality, progress, patriotism, and God, and their attendant virtues of liberty, democracy, individualism, republicanism, and, of course, American expansionism or manifest destiny. "The righteous cause," wrote Holley, "the cause of LIBERTY, PHILANTHROPY, and RELIGION—shall prosper. Such is the cause of Texas." Mexicans, on the other hand, she described as "very indolent, of loose morals, and if not infidels, of which there are many, involved in the grossest superstition." "Mexico can never conquer Texas! The justice and benevolence of Providence will forbid that delightful and now civilized region should again become a howling wilderness," Holley proclaimed. "The Anglo-Saxon American race are destined to be forever the proprietors of this land of promise and fulfillment. Their laws will govern it, their learning will enlighten it, their enterprise will improve it, their flocks alone will range its boundless pastures, for them alone its fertile lands will yield their luxuriant harvests." Texans were protected by "the genius of liberty and sanctified by the spirit of a beneficent religion," and all this was inevitable because "the wilderness of Texas" had been "redeemed by American blood and enterprise."[17]

In her righteous and patriotic fervor, Holley did not neglect the historian's duty to the facts. "You may correct the style, rearrange, leave out the poetry, as you wish," she wrote Orville Holley, whom she enlisted as her agent, "but the facts must go as they are." She obviously intended and believed her account to be objective. "There is no embellishment, no exaggeration," she assured him. Furthermore, she was conscientious in her research. In her trip to Texas in 1831, she had witnessed firsthand the physical features of the country and had interviewed fellow travelers and prominent residents. Being fluent in both Spanish and French, she had read the writings of Lorenzo de Zavala and European travelers to Mexico. Her most valuable source of information, of course, was Stephen F. Austin himself. "I have not only had the benefit of my own observation and experience," she wrote in 1831, "but I have had the assistance of Col. Austin and my brother, Henry, to whom [my manuscript] has been read sheet by sheet, as written. No other individuals are so well acquainted with the subject." When events in late 1835 and 1836 prompted her to mold her erstwhile immigrant guide into what she hoped was an inspiring history, her distance from the scene of the action created some difficulty in collecting accurate data. Nevertheless, with the help of her brother, Henry, and Stephen F. Austin, she acquired many of the official documents relative to Texas and its revolution, which she appended to her manuscript to give it authority.[18]

Without question or pretense to the contrary, the element of Holley's history most characteristic of its time was its utility, a fact she readily admitted.[19] When she spoke of utility directly, she referred to its usefulness to the prospective immigrant. However, Mary Austin Holley never lost sight of the book's usefulness to herself and her family. She knew that Texas, being "terra incognita," was a subject that would capture the attention of the reading public. In December 1831, she wrote to Orville L. Holley in New York: "I have written a book and want it published. . . . It is a work on Texas, and I think a valuable one. . . . I think such a work is wanted and will be well received by the public. I think it will not only do me credit, but, what is quite as good in my circumstances, it may bring me a good sum of money. . . . Such a book is much sought for at the South—a good number should be sent to New Orleans and to Mobile. Also to Kentucky and Cincinnati, Ohio. . . . Your bargain must be for *one edition* only," she cautioned Orville in closing. "They say I would have $1000."[20]

Apparently, Holley's faith in the book's public appeal was not misplaced. In April 1833, she wrote her daughter, Harriette, from New Orleans: "I have a prospect of a large subscription here—say, 200—many paid." In December of that year she confided to Harriette, "They wrote me from New York that my books were in the store of Bogert & Hawthorne. . . . I soon had them in all the book-stores and they are going off very well. . . . There will not be many remaining. I think I may promise myself another edition with profit." She gained notoriety and influence, too, with the publication of her first book on Texas, as she revealed later in the same letter to Harriette: "I dined yesterday with Mrs. Lewis Duncan, and the other day at the French Consul's, an acquaintance made through my *literary fame* [emphasis Holley's], he being a traveller and curious about new countries." She exploited that interest to attract immigrants to Texas, to lionize Stephen F. Austin, and to make money.[21]

No doubt because of her own vested interest in Texas, as well as out of regard for her cousin, Holley determined to help Texas secure recognition by the United States and, perhaps later, annexation, the advantages of which, she believed, far outweighed the dangers of the extension of slavery. Her second book, which appeared in July 1836, sold even better than her first volume. In fact, she exerted an influence not only in Kentucky but also in Texas and in Europe. In November 1836, Henry Austin wrote to her: "Your book is much asked for here and I have ordered 75 copies. . . . It was quoted in Congress a few days ago as authority. . . ."[22]

Hence, the first history of Texas written in English had limited goals. It did not seek primarily to instruct its audience on proper social values, provide lofty intellectual amusement, or explain a culture to itself although Holley did presume to predict the future of Texas as the workings of Providence. It was not written to promote human understanding but to promote individual interests—her interests and those of her family members. If in the process her history memorialized fallen worthies and reinforced basic assumptions about the conduct of life, it did so merely as a reflection of the climate of opinion, the contradictory romantic idealism and materialism of America in the mid-1830s.

One historian whose interest in writing Texas history was obviously influenced by Mary Austin Holley was David Barnett Edward, the self-described "preceptor" of Gonzales Seminary, one of Texas' earliest schools. Edward was "a Scotch Laird" and obviously proud of all that his birthright implied. "I was born . . . in Scotland," he wrote, "that classic land of science and renown, where *a Wallace fought, a Knox preached,* and *a Scott wrote*."[23] Edward possessed a restless spirit prompted, he claimed, by his curiosity about freedom and democracy in the New World. He lived in the West Indies and South America before settling in Louisiana in 1819, where he became principal of the academy in Alexandria. Edward moved to Texas in 1830 and lived there until 1833. He applied for a copyright in 1834 for a manuscript entitled *Observations on Texas, Embracing the Past, the Present, and the Future,* which was to have been published in Alexandria, Louisiana, but apparently never made it into print. According to Edward, he wrote his *History of Texas* (1836) after living there on the frontier for three years, plus a six-month visit in 1835 during which he updated his previous work.[24]

Although precise sales statistics are difficult to determine, Edward's work probably received fairly wide distribution. Cincinnati was an important center of publishing and the book trade in America in the nineteenth century. By the 1830s, it was "the capital of the Western book trade." Available general statistics show that the rate of books published annually in Cincinnati increased from about 350,000 in 1831 to almost 2 million in 1840. Furthermore, J. A. James and Company, Edward's publisher, was among the most important of the Cincinnati publishing houses, "known to everyone in the Mississippi Valley." James and Company was so successful that it became known as "the Harper's of the West." As such, its books would have been widely distributed and promoted.[25]

What precise event inspired Edward to write a history of Texas was not immediately apparent, but two things were evident from his title: Edward's sense that history must have a practical use (hence an immigrant's guide) and his acceptance of the historicist's assumption that for people to be interested in a place, knowledge of its history would be of primary importance. By his own account, he claimed to be writing for the purpose of setting the record straight, "believing that no country or people, so *nearly* allied with the republicans of the North, have ever been less impartially considered; or when spoken of, more unwarrantably exposed to the extremes of *calumny* and *panegyric:* each in its turn creating no little excitement in the breasts of those who are anxious to know of things *just as they are,* before a movement should be made which might bring disappointment, if not ruin, in its train." Whatever his motivations, Edward reassured his readers of his objectivity and insisted from the outset that he was *not* motivated by self-interest, at the same time acknowledging that perfect objectivity might not ingratiate him in some circles. "I have covenanted—let the consequences be what it [*sic*] may—to steer a neutral course, between the extravagant representations of the monopolizing land speculator, and the unwarrantable scurrility of the viciously prejudiced. . . . And to insure the convincement of my reader—I have *no* lands in Texas to sell." Far from profiting by this book, Edward assured his readers, telling the truth had cost him money as well as physical hardships. Nor did he write to advance a political agenda, he contended further, "therefore, may my readers rest assured, that I write with a pen untrammeled by the influence of a *party*," although the assertion in his preface that he had taken "no interest whatsoever in the *political* contests of that country" might well have been, and was, heatedly contested by some of his contemporaries. His sole reason for writing, Edward insisted, was his own amusement and the satisfaction of his friends. [26]

However amused and satisfied he and his friends may have been, Edward's Anglo-American contemporaries in Texas found his rendering of Texas history neither morally uplifting nor amusing, and far from satisfying. He came under severe attack for what was considered his pro-Mexican leanings. The outrage was so intense that Stephen F. Austin narrowly escaped a duel in July 1836 for reputedly accusing John T. Mason of writing it. Mason, a land agent whose business was almost wiped out when the revolutionary government of Texas canceled some large land grants, was highly insulted. He called the book "a slander on the people of Texas" and threatened to "hold [Austin] up as the author of a Slander" for allegedly connecting his name with it. Mason's outrage might have led to blows but for the intervention of Branch T. Archer, who assured him that Austin had made no such remarks regarding the author of the book and accepted responsibility for the matter himself. E. M. Pease is said to have written to his father after the book appeared: "Be cautious of using Edward's *History of Texas.* There is little in his work that can be relied on except what is stolen from Mrs. Holley." Edward found it necessary to leave Texas for good. He moved to Ohio (where his *History* was published) and died there in 1870.[27]

The source of all the commotion was what later critics have referred to as Edward's pro-Mexican politics and "clearly anti-Texan" bias.[28] In point of fact, Edward wrote that he had "every reason to believe and say that the hearts of the actual . . . landholders and farmers, [were] filled with love and gratitude towards their benefactors. . . . Always directed by the motto of their political faith,—*Never ending fidelity to the government of that constitution under which they became privileged citizens*—they voluntarily assume[d] the guardianship of Liberty." *Liberty,* he asserted, was a word that covered many ambiguities and concealed "many of the darkest and most malignant deeds, that have ever debased the character of man," and that had been "wrested by political adventurers and political fanatics to the destruction of thousands; leading them to believe that anarchy was order and party spirit that of patriotism."[29] In short, Edwards contended that Texans were not bad, but out of ignorance, weakness, or naïveté had been duped by self-serving adventurers into a foolish and faithless revolution.

To explain the turbulent political conditions in Mexico and the behavior of its leaders, Edward resorted to the popular use of classical references and compared the Mexican national character to that of Rome after the expulsion of the Tarquins. Like them, he explained, Mexico's leading characters, "having been bred and reared in the lap of war, feel a reluctancy to lay down their military power, and its flattering consequences." With searing logic, Edward defended the Mexican character against Anglo-American presumptions of its inferiority with oblique yet unmistakable reference to United States history, particularly the events of the instant decade. One thing was certain, he asserted: Mexico would never submit to rule by a crowned head again or even for long by an aristocracy because, however they might disagree, "no nation or people will be allowed to interfere; nor *any* State of the present confederation be suffered to withdraw itself *entirely* by violent means, to a state of independence; or by its own negotiation *alone,* place itself under the protection of *any* other government." With this rather sweeping prediction, Edward departed the realm of historical interpretation and revealed the emotional bias of which his Texan detractors had accused him. In his preface, he had made reference to his discouragement over "man's inhumanity to man." Edward alluded to America's own struggle for independence (and possibly to South Carolina's recent threat of secession in 1832–33) as he pointed out bluntly that under the Mexican republic *every* man became a voter at the age of eighteen without discrimination as to property, taxation, or color, "a great improvement upon the federal constitution of America, which acknowledges *all* men as free and equal, yet allows of negro slavery and Indian oppression."[30] Thus, despite his claims to perfect impartiality, Edward clearly used his *History* as a forum for personal moral and political opinions.

It was most certainly, though, Edward's characterization of the people of Texas that provoked the outrage that accompanied publication of his *History of Texas.* He characterized them in general as composed of a class who had been "unfortunate in life," some simply poor and others ne'er-do-wells or lazy opportunists. Another group Edward termed "innovators," unprincipled speculators who sought to receive property of one government while determined, if possible, to belong to another. At the feet of this class of Texas immigrant Edward laid primary responsibility for the problems between the citizens of

Texas and the Mexican government. If one felt compelled to justify their schemes at the expense of their "Republican Mexican benefactors," Edward suggested two possible scenarios: first, the discovery that the true line of demarcation between the United States and Mexico might be laid west of the supposed and acknowledged boundary of 1819 or, second, the knowledge that the Mexican government, desirous of unloading its wayward and unruly province, intended to give it to England in payment of that nation's pecuniary claims against Mexico. Were this indeed the case, Edward conceded with deliberate irony, then Mexico would be responsible for provoking war and bloodshed, because the United States would have to interfere for self-preservation and to avoid being surrounded by that "ambitious, overreaching, and avaricious nation!" Nevertheless, Edward insisted, these avaricious land speculators manipulated both the Texas yeomanry and Stephen F. Austin to the detriment of all involved.[31]

As further indication of his intention to make out of Texas history a moral lesson, Edward took a distinctly sympathetic view of the "savages." Under the influence of early-nineteenth-century romanticism, one might view the American Indian as either "a noble savage" or an uncivilized beast that must be purged from the land in the interest of divinely ordained progress. Edward leaned toward the former attitude while observing fairly that the depredations of the Indians were an understandable and predictable response to the invasion of their domain by white settlers and that the settlers' fear and aversion toward the Indians were predictable and understandable responses to the presence of these unknown people.[32] As the works of Morfi and Pichardo had suggested earlier, in Texas most Indian groups were really remnants of broken tribes, generally disunited among themselves, and, when compared with a Texas full of white settlers, as Edward noted, were "utterly contemptible and harmless." With only a few words, he pointed out that Indians were attracted to Texas for essentially the same reason that white settlers were, noting that the United States' own Indian removal policy accounted for much of what white settlers in Texas perceived as a problem. Because the land left for Indians was generally worthless, Edward observed, it was understandable that they might be attracted to what Texas had to offer in abundance.[33]

Edward, concluding his history prior to the end of Texas' war for independence, performed what many of his contemporaries regarded as the duty of a modern historian and speculated on the probable outcome of the Texian war. He predicted that the most probable and desirable result would be for the States Rights Party of Mexico to overturn the present government and reestablish the Federal Constitution of 1824. This, wrote Edward, would prevent Antonio López de Santa Anna's personal involvement in the affairs of

Texas, which would, in turn, spare trouble and bloodshed; "for he is a 'Jackson' of a fellow, and that speaks volumes to an American." Such a comparison probably did not speak the same volumes to all Americans, but no doubt the audience at whom he directed such remarks would immediately take his meaning, and Edward obviously knew it. A second possible outcome, Edward predicted, might be the laying aside of all other political considerations by Mexico until it completely subdued the Texian Americans and either placed them under military rule or expelled them from the Mexican republic altogether, in which case Texas would surely revert to wilderness. The third and least desirable possibility would be that the government of the United States become involved, with the result a general war between the two republics, an event that Edward clearly believed would corrupt both Texas and Mexico. In his words is much to remind readers of transcendentalist Henry David Thoreau, expounding a decade later on the immorality of the Mexican War.[34]

Having dealt with the themes of morality, progress, and patriotism, Edward turned in his concluding chapter to comments on religion, remarking that "a true historian should be faithful to the trust reposed in him by all who come within the sphere of his observations." In this as in other aspects of his account of Texas, Edward endeavored to represent both Texan and Mexican. He generalized about both by admonishing against hypocrisy and the abuse of religion for self-aggrandizement or political ends. "'The work of the Lord' being their watch word, but 'worldly ease' their rallying point!" he accused.[35] He critically examined the virtues of liberty and republicanism with an equally balanced presentation of the pros and cons.

Edward wrote with little of the drama and color he might have admired in the writing of Sir Walter Scott, apparently determined to bolster his objectivity by eschewing excess either in words or emotion. Nevertheless, in describing that portion of Texas lying between the Sabine and Trinity Rivers, Edward waxed as eloquent as any romantic writer or Texas historian before him. "Few spectacles surpass it in beauty and magnificence," he wrote. "Nature invites the cultures of art with the most alluring smiles." He subsequently compared his first glimpse of the valley of the Guadalupe to that of Moses beholding the land of Canaan, and he last compared the reality of Texas to "those fabled dreams of the Elysian fields."[36]

For authority Edward relied heavily on his own firsthand observations. Such observations he considered sufficient qualification for writing a history since "throughout thirty years experience in the busy world" he had been "brought to such a measure of thought as to judge cautiously, charitably, and in some degree philanthropically of the actions of men." In addition to his reliance on his own judgment and despite his unfortunate plagiarism of some secondary sources, Edward did not neglect the collection and study of primary sources. He quoted full texts of or important extracts from Mexican laws and regulations regarding colonization policy, judicial system, and trade, many of which were never included elsewhere. He provided the full text of the proposed Constitution of 1833 and many other official documents of both sides between 1832 and 1835. An appendix contained census statistics for North America, Mexico, and South America, and an English translation of the Mexican Constitution of 1824. As a result, Edward's *History of Texas* has been described by twentieth-century bibliographers as "one of the best accounts of Texas on the eve of the revolution" and "one of the few choice early histories of Texas."[37]

Actually, despite his eloquent explanation of his purpose and his claims of impartiality, Edward did, indeed, have a personal agenda. According to a family memorial, written in part by Edward himself, he attributed a "family" loss of twenty thousand dollars to "the slaveholding *unjust* Texian war of 1836." He undertook his sojourns in the Indies and South America, it seems, in pursuit of his brother, James, who had lost a twenty-thousand-dollar family inheritance in the New York Stock Exchange. Having lost his farm in Virginia to debt as a result, David Edward eventually went to Mexico and acquired 640 acres of land under Mexican laws, which he lost, in turn, when Texas won its independence.[38] Thus, David Barnett Edward became Texas' first revisionist historian but with a purpose no less personal than those of promoters like the Austins or Mary Holley.

Even as Edward's book ended, the apparent success of the Texas Revolution merely increased popular interest in the subject and prompted a virtual frenzy of writing and publication. One of the earliest books purporting to be a history was the *History of the Revolution in Texas, Particularly of the War of 1835 & '36; Together with the Latest Geographical, Topographical, and Statistical Accounts of the Country, from the Most Authentic Sources* by Chester Newell, Massachusetts native, Episcopal minister, and Yale graduate, who came to Texas for his health in the spring of 1837. According to the editors of *The Writings of Sam Houston,* he hoped to defray his expenses by writing a history. He resided in Texas for a year, three months of which he spent in the capital of the republic acquiring the information and material necessary to write his history. In fact, Newell purchased land on the Lavaca River and also obtained a headright grant that he had to return to Texas to perfect. He wrote to Samuel May Williams in September 1838 requesting funds with which to return to Texas and pledging sales of his book as security: "Can you aid me in getting to Texas . . . by advancing me a small sum, say enough to get to

Cincinnati, and become security for me to the amount of two or three hundred copies of my work on Texas, that I may take the same along, and, perhaps, beside paying the cost, pay my passage by the sale of them? (I am obliged to purchase, (at the rate of fifty cents a copy) my work. . . . I sell the same for one dollar, and thus, where I can dispose of several, realise [*sic*] a good profit.)"[39]

Newell cited as sources documents in the War Department and "others to which he had access" and interviews with several distinguished participants in the war, including Sam Houston and Mirabeau Lamar. Newell described his method as "studied conciseness and perspicuity, more than elegance," as he sought to be "useful" rather than original, assuring his public that he had chiefly endeavored to "exhibit the truth" in all that he had written.[40] He started with a year-by-year recitation of the history of Mexico from 1821 to 1835, beginning with the revolt of Colonel Agustín de Iturbide and ending with the centralization and consolidation of the government under Santa Anna in June 1835. This he drew from the accounts of witnesses and from previously published Mexican accounts, adding virtually no editorial comment whatsoever.[41]

To be purely objective throughout, however, Newell would have had to resist interpretation, and that was not his purpose. In the dedication of his book to the Honorable W. C. Preston of South Carolina, Newell portrayed the people of Texas as "oppressed and calumniated." He obviously made it his purpose to vindicate their character and their cause. The Texan Revolution, Newell wanted the American public to know, was a victory for the romantic principles of morality, God, and progress, and the virtues of liberty, individualism, and expansion of the Anglo-American race. With rapturous references to classical Italy, destiny, the redemption of the uncivilized wilderness, and Anglo-American superiority, Newell portrayed Texas as every bit the second Eden his predecessors had.[42] He dutifully described the geography, topography, statistics, and towns of the republic, and he analyzed the people and projected the future of the region.

Newell claimed that his principal object in writing was "faithfully and impartially to exhibit the causes and narrate the interesting events of the Revolution." Having purchased a league of land there himself, though, he had something of a personal interest in writing a history to promote the interests of Texas as an independent nation.[43] In any event, Newell presented a patently pro-Texan version of the "truth" that emphasized repeatedly Spain's and, subsequently, Mexico's use, abuse, and oppression of foreign immigrants to compensate for their own respective ineptitude and inability to protect and develop the province. In the first two chapters alone, Newell managed to make at least one reference on every page to the rights of the colonists and Mexican violations of same. Newell, like Holley before him, described the conflict between Mexico and its Texas colonists as the inevitable result of utterly incompatible and unresolvable cultural differences. Comparing the "licentious character" of the soldiers of Mexico with the character of North Americans, "obedient to law, and universally jealous of their rights," Newell concluded, "it must be perfectly evident that Mexican soldiers and North American citizens could not live together without collision." Newell viewed the colonists themselves, not as the indigents, criminals, and opportunists Edward had painted them but as people "tired and disgusted . . . with the noise and rancor of party strife in the United States" who had immigrated to Texas in search of peace and quiet, better soil, and a milder climate. If some of them had been "carried to some extremes in manner and in measures," it was only because the determined spirit of their race had been justifiably aroused in defense of liberty. He seemed, as much as anything, determined to redeem the reputation of the Texans by the writing of their history. "There is existing in the minds of the people in many places, if not generally, at the North, a strong and bitter prejudice against Texas," he wrote. The majority of Texans could not possibly be of such a poor character, he argued; otherwise, "how could they have achieved their Independence and established a regular and efficient government?" And even if a large part of them were miscreants and ne'er-do-wells, he asked the reader, "should the entire population and country be then reviled?" Moreover, Newell never missed an opportunity to emphasize the chivalry of Texan leaders, such as Fannin, and the "chivalrous and generous spirit" of the companies of volunteers in the cause of Texas.[44]

Newell did not disappoint those who believed it the duty of historians to immerse the reader in the scene and make history dramatic and picturesque. Influenced by the historical fiction of Sir Walter Scott, by far the best-selling author in the United States before the Civil War, Newell's readers expected as much from their historians as from a novelist. Scott heightened the effect of history with the high adventure and emotional warmth of fiction, and he awakened public interest in history on an unprecedented scale. Newell was aware that American historians who succeeded in capturing the attention and interest of their compatriots in historical subjects strove to emulate Scott. He described with relish "the shrill sound of the fife, the soul-stiffing beat of the drum, and flash of the bright sun on the rifles." He faithfully portrayed the Texans as heroes in a sublime battle for God, liberty, and the American way. With vivid simile, he recounted James Fannin's loss at Goliad, assuring his readers that the independence of Texas was secured by these hapless men, whose blood "like dragon's teeth, sown upon the earth" caused others to rise and rush into battle.[45]

In background, occupation, style, theme, method, and even motivation, Newell fitted the mold of American romantic historians. Like many of them, he realized little or no monetary gain directly from the sale of his book. On the contrary, he incurred the cost of publishing it himself. Like others who wrote about Texas, he had personal, practical reasons for promoting the newly formed republic. Reviewers, particularly those whose interest in the Texas republic conflicted with his, labeled his work propaganda and harshly criticized Newell for his partisanship despite his claim to truth and impartiality.[46]

Newell and his fellow writers had an audience both in the United States and on the other side of the Atlantic. Newell's publisher, Wiley and Putnam, at the time a major New York publishing house, boasted a London branch as well, mainly devoted to bookselling.[47] As demonstrated by the prompt appearance of a review of Newell's book abroad, Europeans had as lively a curiosity as Americans about the affairs of Texas, particularly once it had separated itself from Mexico. Part of this fascination may have stemmed from the romantic impulses of the age, but part of it undoubtedly had more to do with European economic interests of one kind or another. By all accounts, the Frenchman Frédéric LeClerc was inspired by the former; however, considering the number of Europeans visiting and writing about America in the early nineteenth century, it seems likely that LeClerc's intellectual curiosity had been piqued, like that of Alexis de Tocqueville, Harriet Martineau, and Frances Trollope, by the United States' peculiar revolution and democratic experiment, and by the Anglo-Americans' aggressive definition of liberty in comparison with the French experience. LeClerc, in the opening remarks to his book on Texas, admitted that the recurrence of this revolutionary phenomenon in Texas and the potential impact that an independent country of such tremendous resources would have on the world prompted European interest in the new republic.[48]

Frédéric LeClerc, a French physician, came to Texas in 1838. He had been educated at the University of Paris and belonged to a number of learned societies, including the Society of Natural History and Entomological Society of France. Like Darby's report and a great many other works published at the time, LeClerc's effort first appeared serialized in a periodical. His short history of the Texas Revolution was originally published in *La Revue des Deux-Mondes* in two installments (March 1 and April 15, 1840), but an English translation soon appeared before American readers in the *Southern Literary Messenger*.[49]

Following the typical pattern, LeClerc opened his history with a description of the rivers, soil, and people of Texas in order to lend scientific credibility to the work and to facilitate the reader's understanding of the historical events about to be related. He dismissed the question of Texas' discovery by Europeans as difficult to determine precisely and "not really very important to know" but made it clear that he had researched his subject, referring to the journey of Cabeza de Vaca "towards 1536" and a manuscript history of the new kingdom of Galicia written in 1742. Like Morfi and Pichardo, he acknowledged that, had La Salle's colony not perished, Texas might very well have been French. He was not the first, nor would he be the last, but LeClerc was among those critical historians of the nineteenth century who argued the inevitability of the Texas Revolution given Spain's neglect of the province's obvious attributes and the proximity of the United States and the Anglo-American race. "Indeed, the consequences of their proximity were not long in developing," he wrote, "and the European political picture, always a great factor in the destiny of the New World, was to accelerate the trend towards revolution." Further, he unmistakably understood the implications of the advance of the Anglo-Americans into Texas:

> The natural resources of the land, the good climate, the possibility of instituting steam navigation on its rivers, were facts well known throughout the Union and especially in the new Western and Southern states. . . . Texas . . . offered an almost limitless field to slave labor, one practically boundless both in area and in types of agriculture which might prove profitable, on its rich virgin plains. By extending its frontier to the Rio Grande, the United States would have drawn considerably nearer to the great mining regions; and to several Mexican provinces whose population, already well-established, rather wealthy, and devoid of industries, would have constituted a valuable market for its commerce. Finally, one step more would have been taken, and a very important step, towards the Sea of California and the Pacific Ocean, so laboriously reached much farther north, by means of the difficult Rocky Mountain passes, and the sandy deserts to their west.[50]

Thus, LeClerc realized fully all the material, practical reasons why the United States would be aggressive toward Texas and at the same time acknowledged the age-old myth of westward migration: the search for a route to the East, pulling western Europeans like a magnet over the centuries. Neither did he fail to appreciate the effect Andrew Jackson's personality had on the climate of opinion. "Jackson seemed destined to extend into what was formerly Spanish territory the empire of that aggressive race whose passions and indomitable instincts he shares," he observed.[51] After concluding his introductory chapters by commenting on the speed with which the Anglo-American race had obtained first the mouth of the Mississippi and then Texas, he proceeded to the main subject of his writing, the history of the Texas Revolution itself.

LeClerc proffered several causes for the trouble between Mexico and its Texas colonists, but the two he emphasized were the diplomatic pressures of both the United States and England. He noted that some in the Mexican republic believed the United States had aided Spain in the Barbados expedition, the last Spanish threat to Mexican independence, and were further convinced of the American threat by American diplomat Joel Poinsett's overtures to acquire Texas while he served as the first United States minister to Mexico from 1825 to 1829. He attributed much disquiet on the part of the United States to President Vicente Guerrero's abolition of slavery in Mexico in 1829, because of the sensation it might produce among slaves of the southern United States, especially when Poinsett learned that Guerrero was contemplating the fostering of a slave revolt in Cuba. And LeClerc noted that English influence probably had something to do with Mexican hostility toward the United States. In addition, he pointed out that proclaiming the immediate abolition of slavery in all parts of Mexico was undeniably a breach of faith toward the Texas colonists and would have ruined the settlers of Texas had provincial governor Viesca not insisted on its repeal where Texas was concerned. He surmised that attacks on the Mexican character in American newspapers in the latter part of 1829 probably did not help matters. Also to be considered was the ambition of Stephen F. Austin, whom he portrayed as a conniver bent on obtaining commercial control of the northern province of the Mexican federation, including Chihuahua and ultimately Santa Fe. American ambition aside, LeClerc concluded that Americans were simply in a revolutionary mood. He cited a Louisiana newspaper announcement that Sam Houston was going to Texas in late 1829 or in 1830 to "revolutionize" the land. "Let it be noted in passing," he wrote, "the proof which this offers of the strong revolutionary element contributing so heavily to the settling of Texas, proof of the inevitability of the explosion." He conceded that beyond American aggressiveness, the turmoil of the Mexican government contributed in no small measure to the trouble in Texas. He cited constant civil wars, lack of discipline among government troops stationed in Texas, and the chronic distrust of the Mexican government as factors that, combined with the Anglo-American instinct toward self-government, forced the Texans to their decision "irresistibly."[52]

LeClerc maintained his attitude of detached observer throughout his account and analysis of the war for Texas independence itself and the subsequent development of the Texas republic. Although he drew largely from previously published works such as Barbe-Marbois's *History of Louisiana* and Newell's *History of the Revolution in Texas,* he relied, fortunately, on astute personal observation and his own remarkable political insight, going so far as to point out inconsistencies between Newell's account and the evidence of original documents. LeClerc made concise analyses of both events and personalities, presenting the leading figures with an even hand. He obviously respected Austin for his good sense and disrespected Houston for his "unsoldierly deportment" and "undignified manners." In fairness, however, he wrote, "One is wrong to blame General Houston for not facing the enemy any sooner. On the Colorado and even on the Brazos he did not have a single cannon. In proportion as he withdrew, he concentrated to better advantage all the forces at his command, whereas Santa Anna continually left some of his troops along the way; and there is reason to believe that by drawing nearer the United States border he was counting on some help, at least indirect, from General Gaines. . . ."[53] LeClerc refrained from treating the Texans as larger than life, appearing neither particularly sympathetic nor antipathetic to their cause. Of Texans and the Anglo-American race in general he seemed simply awed—by their ambition, by their determination, by their rather foolish bravado, and, in spite of it all, by their accomplishments.

Frédéric LeClerc demonstrated that romantic history could be and sometimes was analytical and objective. Although drawn to his subject at least partly because of its obvious interest and appeal to the reading public, he did not seek to expound any great themes or teach any great moral lessons but merely to shed the light of insight on events that had attracted the world's attention. Furthermore, he did so with apparent conciseness and without the hyperbole that frequently characterized the romantic era. He returned to France after his visit to Texas and continued his career as a distinguished physician. He did return to the United States to live in 1872, but not to Texas. He died in Bloomfield, New Mexico, in 1891.[54]

As the decade of the 1830s drew to a close on the newly formed and highly controversial Republic of Texas, one other history-cum-immigrant guide found its way into print in America. Hardly a patrician, its author, Edward Stiff, a Virginian by birth, had occupied himself as a hatter in Baltimore, Maryland, before making a visit to Texas in 1839. He claimed to be motivated by "combined causes," the precise nature of which he failed to elaborate, but primarily for the purpose of preparing an immigrant guide for the common man at whom, in his opinion, no previous such works had been directed. He also asserted, as had virtually all of his predecessors, that his work was needed because no works on Texas had yet been written "with that independence of thought, and strict impartiality, which should ever be the aim and end of the Historian who aspires to an enduring and honourable fame." This allusion to himself as "historian," in addition to the statement that he had included "other and dissimilar information" as well as that necessary to guide immigrants, distinguished Stiff's work from other contemporary travel books and guides. Despite his claim to perfect impartiality, Stiff clearly had strong opinions about Texas and believed that his interpretation of the Texas situation would interest and benefit many Americans who, he perceived, had an avid interest in it, possibly as much from a political standpoint as from an immigrant's: "[The author] frankly acknowledges that he is and has been determined to express his own opinions; to wear all the honours and bear all the obloquy which this volume may call forth," Stiff warned in his preface.[55]

The reason for such a caveat became evident in the course of Stiff's writing. Although his work has been praised as one of the most objective contemporary accounts, it was heavily slanted toward the Mexican government and against the "war party" in Texas, in which Stiff included everyone who supported independence from Mexico. Further, Stiff's interpretation might have been influenced by his own political troubles during his stay in Texas. His book contained a number of unflattering references to Houston's mayor and editor of the *Telegraph and Texas Register*, Francis Moore Jr., who appointed Stiff deputy constable in Houston only to discharge him twice from the office for drunkenness.[56]

Actually, Stiff's admitted interest in national politics, despite local hard feelings, might ultimately have been what prompted his attention to all sides of the Texas question in his writing, thus earning him credit among later historians and bibliographers for his objectivity:

> There has [*sic*] always been those among us who have viewed [Texas] with a wishful eye, a feeling in which the government have [*sic*] at times participated. . . . Again, there is, and has long been many of our citizens who view a further extension of territory as dangerous to the integrity of the Union, and have constantly manifested a determined opposition to measures of such tendency; and while our party have invariably asserted that in fixing the Sabine as the south western boundary of the United States, the American Secretary was outwitted by Don Ennis de Onís, the Spanish Minister. Others, with perhaps equal information, have ascribed to the Hon. John Q. Adams, motives wholly unworthy of an American Statesman.[57]

Since Edward Stiff apparently remained in Texas for only about sixty days, much of his information was of necessity gleaned from secondary sources, though he insisted his work was itself original: "[I]f the Author has studied, it has been to produce an original and correct picture. He has selected no model . . . if, under such circumstances, it were impossible to avoid colours which may have been used before, it is not the result of a mind affected with the spirit of plagiarism, but the natural offspring of desultory reading, and intercourse with the world, and that sort of instinct which has at all times imperceptibly drawn him away from fixed fashions and rules."[58]

If by "fashions and rules" Stiff referred to flowery romantic literary style, he spoke truthfully. Even though he sometimes wrote with exaggerated formality, he rarely engaged in the hyperbole often associated with romantic literature. Nor did he become carried away with heroes and villains. Stiff waxed poetic, however, in describing the land itself and the amazing outcome of the battle of San Jacinto. "No traveler can cast his eye over this plain without calling to mind the prodigious results that sometimes flow from comparative small causes, and certainly no American can pass the spot without feeling a flow of manly pride at the remembrance of the deeds of valour performed by the Spartan band of San Jacinto," he wrote. With frank acknowledgment of the differences of opinion over the Texas Revolution, Stiff noted that whether the Americans who fought there had been misinformed or not, the prompting motive was a noble one and should have earned them the respect of those who had claimed to espouse the cause of freedom in the world.[59] Like Frédéric LeClerc and others, Stiff was impressed by the fact that these people could not only face but overcome such tremendous odds, and he willingly assumed that such a feat could stem only from noble intentions.

Though Stiff's warmth toward the Texan army might not have been shared by all his contemporaries, his attitude toward the land itself reiterated the myth of Texas as the Promised Land. "Even here," he reflected, "far removed from civilization, the hand of a beneficen [sic], Being could be easily traced and his promises to the fatherless and widow realised." In this, Stiff did not measurably differ from the Spanish clerics Morfi and Pichardo, from the Puritans who sought to redeem the faith of the Old World in the New, from the myths and legends that grew out of the rumored settlement of Portuguese priests in the Antilles before the voyages of Columbus, or, for that matter, from the beginning of the Judeo-Christian tradition. American tradition, especially, had attached moral and cultural significance to the land. To Stiff, as to his predecessors and to his readers, Texas represented the opportunity to start afresh, to redeem failures, to succeed.[60]

That Edward Stiff regarded his work as a history as well as a guide for immigrants became even clearer when he republished it virtually unchanged, except for the addition of documents related to the Mexican War, as *A New History of Texas; From the First European Settlement in 1692, Down to the Pre-*

sent Time . . . in 1848. Although it is impossible to determine with any precision how widely it was read, the fact that Stiff's book was republished by the same publisher, George Conclin, one of the two most prominent publishers in the Cincinnati book trade, suggests that it was reasonably successful. George Conclin was a key promoter of trade sales, the purpose of which was to facilitate the exchange of books published in different sections of the country by exhibiting them at fairs and taking orders for them.[61]

A number of other works by Americans and Europeans appeared in the years between the War of 1812 and 1840 that sought to take advantage of the great public interest in Texas and its revolution. Nearly all included some comments on Texas' history. Immigrant guides, such as those published by Detlef Dunt in 1834, and travelogues, such as Amos Andrew Parker's *A Trip to the West and Texas* (1835) and the anonymously published *A Visit to Texas* (1834), provided much useful information, insights, and often vivid contemporary accounts of Texas as the writers found it, but they emphasized what Texas was, its present and future prospects, not how it had come to be. Other books written during the same period offered personal accounts of specific events, such as the French writers Hartmann and Millard's diary account of Napoleonic refugees in Texas or Robert M. Coleman's diatribe against Sam Houston's handling of the San Jacinto campaign.[62] Though their purposes for writing might have been similar to those of other writers of Texas history, their primary (and often singular) source of information was their own experience and observation rather than accumulated written and oral documentation.

All diarists, travel writers, promoters, speculators, and self-professed historians of Texas in the early years of the nineteenth century had in common practical motivations for writing about Texas. They took advantage of the avid public interest in that territory to generate a bit of income for themselves, to promote a political agenda, and even to avenge themselves of some real or imagined loss or injustice. Few wrote solely for a higher purpose, such as the dissemination of truth, moral instruction, the demonstration of an ultimate reality, or even pure entertainment. Those who claimed for their work the distinction of "history" were no more consistent in their approaches to that genre than historians and critics elsewhere in America during the romantic era. Their works represented a combination of passion and reason. All the ingredients for romantic history abounded in Texas: turbulent action, scenes of dramatic crisis, battle, and violence, "food for admiration and abhorrence."[63] Yet, of the histories of Texas written up to 1840, only one resorted to blood, thunder, and flowery rhetoric as the primary means of creating interest, and all of them spoke of the landscape in "painterly" terms. With rare exception, they conscientiously sought and relied on primary sources, both written and oral, as well as personal observation, and most were methodical and critical in their presentations of them, only one being essentially narrative. They all ardently proclaimed their impartiality and objectivity, but none achieved it completely. Taken as a whole, however, perhaps they did provide a fairly balanced analysis of Texas history through the war of independence from Mexico. For every history that expressed an Anglo-Texan bias, another exhibited a sharply pro-Mexican stance. Some made heroes of Sam Houston and the Alamo defenders, whereas others cast aspersions on the character of Texans in general and the revolutionists in particular. They perpetuated only one myth with uniformity, that being the enduring perception of the untamed wilderness as humanity's second chance at Eden, probably because it was ingrained in their collective psyche and because that's what all of them were looking for themselves in one way or another.

The most prominent writers of Texas history during this period largely fitted the profile of the patrician historian, but as a group, they reflected more accurately the spirit of the Jacksonian age. They were journalists, teachers, ministers, physicians, of genteel background and classical education, yet at least one was a shopkeeper, a common man, writing for "the common man." They visited Texas out of curiosity and the hope of financial gain; none of them maintained permanent residence there. They exhibited typically romantic themes in their writing, most notably morality, progress, Providence, and the virtues of liberty, democracy, patriotism, and individualism. Nevertheless, the illustration of these themes was secondary to the promotion of personal or political interests. Thus, from the start of Anglo-American historiography of the region, Texas was to its historians more than a place, a land, or an environment. It was a place linked to a utilitarian, functional history. These self-styled historians wrote to sway a contemporary audience, not to benefit a future one.

3 ⋆ Texas Historians *and the* Rise of the Lone Star

Attention had focused on colonization and revolution in Texas during the 1830s, but it turned to the political and diplomatic fortunes of the new republic in the 1840s. Controversy, far from quieting after Texas claimed its independence, increased after the revolution. Mexico's loss of such a large piece of real estate with its attendant resources had a devastating effect on that country's investors, many of whom were English. When initial efforts to annex Texas to the United States failed in 1837 and 1838, the contest for the republic, both at home and abroad, escalated rapidly. The volume of publication on Texas increased proportionately, all of it aimed at persuasion. Much of it, as in the previous decade, donned the respectable and popular cloak of history.

One Texan convinced of the utility of history for promoting his vision for Texas, and his political agenda for achieving it, was Mirabeau B. Lamar, president of the Republic of Texas from 1838 through 1841. Lamar had, from his youth, mingled literature and politics. Moreover, possessing the heart and soul of a poet, he approached both with genuine romantic passion. He had been a politician and newspaper editor in Georgia prior to coming to Texas in 1835 with the idea, among other things, of writing a history of the region, and to that end he amassed a wealth of documentary material.[1] Though circumstances prevented his carrying out the writing himself, when he determined to secure Texas' sovereignty and economic independence, he promptly sought to procure the writing of a history that would bolster his efforts to obtain diplomatic recognition for the republic. In this endeavor he had two likely prospects, William Kennedy, an English diplomat, and Henry Stuart Foote, a writer and politician from Mississippi.

Kennedy became interested in Texas in 1836 after reading newspaper accounts of the province's revolt against Mexico. As in the case of Frédéric

LeClerc and others, Kennedy was intrigued by the fact that this Anglo-American band, so insignificant in number compared with the population of Mexico, had been successful in establishing their independence by force of arms. "I could not clearly understand," he wrote, "how the settlers of Texas were enabled to repel the armies of Mexico and to found a Republic of their own."[2] As he was an Englishman, perhaps his interest had been piqued by the fact that these Americans had been able to repeat this feat no less than three times in fifty years, not only against the larger force of Mexico but twice against England, the mightiest nation on earth.

In fact, William Kennedy's interest in writing and in America predated the Texas Revolution by several years. At the age of twenty-five he had published a volume of prose narrative, and during 1828–29 he had collaborated in the publication of *The Paisley Magazine,* a short-lived periodical. As private secretary to the Earl of Durham, he had accompanied that British political leader to North America to investigate the cause of the Canadian Rebellion. Having become intrigued with what he had read about Texas, Kennedy welcomed the opportunity to satisfy his curiosity firsthand when the Earl of Durham proposed that he visit North America to head a commission for improving municipal institutions in Lower Canada.[3]

After completing his report at the end of 1838, Kennedy set out to satisfy his curiosity about the United States and Texas. He made his way to Texas in 1839 and remained until June, during which time he was warmly received. He was also very favorably impressed with the sanguine attitude of the Texans toward his own country, especially in comparison to the animosity he had encountered toward England in the northern United States. Perhaps this hospitality was responsible for Kennedy's sympathetic attitude toward Texas. Nothing in his correspondence with various individuals nor in the "Personal Narrative" with which he prefaced his book indicated that his interest in Texas at the time stemmed from anything other than curiosity. By 1841, when his book first appeared, Kennedy was clearly concerned for British interests in Texas, which he perceived to be threatened by both France and the United States; thus, one could surmise that he had written his pro-Texan account to encourage and hasten the signing of commercial treaties between England and Texas. In a letter to Lord Aberdeen in October 1841, Kennedy drew attention to remarks on the northwestern boundary question, published in the *London Times,* which he wrote "for the purpose of awakening attention to the subject of American encroachment in that quarter, being thoroughly convinced that, unless English influence be employed in raising up a stable independent power on the South-Western and North-Western frontiers of the Union, a very few years will suffice to place the whole of the territory they covet under the Sovereignty of the United States. *There* lies the danger to the Maritime and Commercial supremacy of Great Britain," he warned. In a later missive, Kennedy took credit for staving off the annexation of Texas to the United States "until the dispositions of Great Britain could be known." Thus, one might conclude that Kennedy sought some personal recognition as a national hero of sorts through his writing even though these sentiments, expressed two or three years following his initial trip, seem more closely related to his diplomatic post as British consul for Texas than to his book. One might also speculate that he intended with his history to generate interest in Texas in anticipation of the promotion of his own colonizing effort in 1842, but there appears to be no evidence that he had conceived of that venture as early as 1839.[4] In any event, Kennedy's interest in writing about Texas became a resolve to promote the republic and its history in England. He immediately commenced collecting documentation, readily assisted by Lamar and his cabinet members. Suitably impressed with Kennedy, Lamar provided access to the collection of historical material he had amassed for the writing of a history. On the eve of his departure, Kennedy met with Lamar and accepted a message from him to the rulers of Great Britain, as well as a letter of introduction to General James Hamilton, who was already on his way to Europe as financial agent for the Republic of Texas. Kennedy returned to England where he continued his correspondence with Mirabeau Lamar. In September 1839, he reassured Lamar that he would exert himself strenuously to bring out his intended work on Texas before the meeting of Parliament in February. "The work of itself will form a defence of Ministers," he wrote, "if they should have the courage and foresight to establish friendly relations with a people whose interests must always be coincident with our own." He promised Lamar copies of the book as soon as it was published.[5]

Whatever his motives or biases, within two years' time, William Kennedy produced the most thorough, comprehensive account of Texas history up to that time, one that set a standard for years to come. Its contemporary influence was profound. It succeeded in its purpose, for it proved a key element in determining England's ultimate recognition of Texas independence. American critics wrote that "a fuller and more satisfactory answer" to the question of the recognition of Texas as an independent republic "is given by Mr. Kennedy, in the work whose title we have just cited, than in any one which has come to our knowledge. The high character of this gentleman, and the fact that he has no personal interests to advance by what he writes, add great weight to his testimony. We hope to see Mr. Kennedy's book reprinted here immediately, feeling confident it will do more to correct the erroneous impressions in regard to Texas, which are prevailing amongst us, than could be done by any other means."[6] Later in the nineteenth century, Homer S. Thrall, author of Texas history schoolbooks, remarked on Kennedy's amazing knowledge of the country and its institutions. "His style is clear; his facts well arranged; his descriptions of the country just and striking." Frank Brown, in the *Annals of Travis County and of the City of Austin (From the Earliest Times to the Close of 1875),* called Kennedy's work "one of the best of the many histories of Texas that have been published from time to time during the past seventy years." More than three-quarters of a century after Kennedy's book appeared, twentieth-century Texas historian Eugene C. Barker acknowledged that Kennedy "wrote with real historical spirit, and in some respects, his book has not been superceded [*sic*]."[7]

Kennedy, like other writers of Texas history in the first half of the nineteenth century, after prefatory remarks, began his work by introducing the reader to the geography, natural history, climate, and topography of Texas. And, like his predecessors, he effused in terms of the age-old myth of the New World Garden along with the more recent emendations to it of the racial principles of Anglo-American expansionism: "Nature has lavished her bounties with the munificence of an indulgent parent; it only remains for man to show himself worthy of her favours, by the due application of his energies, mental and corporeal, and the temperate use of the means of enjoyment placed at his disposal. For a sensual, indolent, uninquiring race, the bowers of a second Eden would bloom in vain." As he dealt with the Spanish and Mexican claims, he similarly dismissed the native Indian tribes as neither having any fixed habitation in Texas nor possessing "that real interest in the land which is derived from labour expended in its cultivation."[8]

Kennedy turned to history to explain the events that had brought Texas to its present state in 1839. He reviewed the history of the Spanish claim as well as the French, carefully documenting his sources in footnotes. He concurred with those who explained the Texas Revolution in terms of an inevitable conflict of cultures and, perhaps more important, of moral principles. He attributed much of the trouble between the Mexicans and their colonists to differences in political background and experience in addition to differences in character and social position. "It were equally futile to expect the practical development of an enlightened polity from a long oppressed, demoralized, and uninstructed people, as to hope for a judicious household economy under the domestic rule of a neglected nursling."[9]

Although Kennedy's sympathy toward the participants in the Gutiérrez-Magee expedition might appear illustrative of a romantic predisposition for adventure, he was probably making a perceptive, realistic observation when he characterized the Americans who joined the expedition as "brave and ar-

dent spirits, to whom the excitement of military adventure was irresistibly at-
tractive." Most of the invading force, he noted, were "in the season of youth-
ful daring," motivated by thrills, not principles. He was equally pragmatic in
his judgment of Stephen F. Austin, noting that his sole recompense depended
on the successful discharge of the responsibilities he had undertaken both to
the colonists and to the Mexican government. On every page, he referred to
copious sources, both primary and secondary, making it evident that he had
read the work of other historians on the subject, was aware of varying interpretations, and corrected inconsistencies. In his account of the surrender of
General Martín Perfecto de Cos, he noted that he had seen the losses estimated at 200 killed and 390 wounded, but that this seemed to be an exaggeration. Further, he observed that Chester Newell claimed twice the number
of men in James Fannin's detachment under Captain Amon B. King at Refu-
gio as General José Urrea had reported in his diary and that he could find no
account of any escaping.[10] Kennedy thus apparently felt no obligation to embellish, exaggerate, or omit facts for the sake of telling a good story.

Like the work of other historians of the romantic period, Kennedy's work
exhibited a distinctly moral tone and typically romantic themes, particularly
the themes of liberty and the superiority of the Anglo-Saxon race. "With the
degenerate races of the South," he wrote, "liberty was but a poetical abstrac-
tion. . . . with the Anglo-Americans it was a substantial inheritance—dear to
them as the memory of their ancestors—essential to their social progress as
the air of heaven to their physical existence." His thorough study of the materials of Texas history did nothing to dissuade him from his original fascination and awe with the unique "go-ahead" character of Americans. "It is the
facility with which the Anglo-Americans mould themselves to circumstances,
whatever they may be, added to their habits of reflection and self-reliance,
that accounts for their pre-eminence in colonization," he concluded.[11]

Though not generally inclined to flowery prose, Kennedy's account of the
battle for the Alamo was worthy of romantic drama, and he waxed especially
poetic in his description of Davy Crockett. In doing so, however, Kennedy,
might well have emphasized a salient point. The notions of the Alamo defenders themselves were even more romantic than romantic historians or
journalists painted them. Without either excusing their behavior or lionizing
them, Kennedy suggested that Crockett, William Travis, Jim Bowie, and others became so carried away by the romantic idea of dying for a cause that they
threw themselves into a ridiculously lopsided battle and actually died for
glory, having ultimately left themselves no other choice.[12]

Although his writing was certainly influenced by romantic style and
themes, William Kennedy exhibited a methodology and honesty of percep-

tion undeserving of late-twentieth-century accusations that his was an adventure story in the guise of history. Although critics point to his vividly
drawn description of a storm at night on the Gulf of Mexico as evidence of
this adventurous perspective, Kennedy's description probably owed more to
very real awe at the terrifying force of nature and his own helplessness in the
face of it than to any peculiar sense of romantic adventure. He included it not
because it had any bearing on Texas history but because it made a vivid impression on him. Moreover, such descriptive style was not confined to formal
writing. It was typical of Kennedy's personal correspondence as well. "Come
to Galveston," he wrote to Anson Jones, "and inhale breezes freshened by
the influences of Neptune."[13] Kennedy's history was consistent with the best
of national writing at the time. Though it was primarily narrative, he interspersed it liberally with excerpts of original documents and commentary on
discrepancies he found in sources and earlier interpretations. He emphasized
the abstract principles behind major actions and the importance of national
character, race, and great men. With as much historical evidence at his disposal as had ever been amassed on Texas history, he interpreted it as proof that
right principles triumph, and those who were wise and practical would ally
themselves with proven winners.

At about the same time he entertained William Kennedy, Lamar entered
into communications with Henry Stuart Foote, a member of the Mississippi
House of Representatives. Originally from Virginia, Foote had been educated
at Georgetown College and Washington University, had studied law, and had
been admitted to the bar. Prior to his election to the Mississippi legislature,
he had occupied himself as a lawyer and newspaper editor in Alabama and
Mississippi.[14] Although it is unclear who first approached Foote, there is no
doubt that he was solicited to write a history of Texas. In the preface to his
first volume, he wrote, "I chanced to visit the Republic of Texas, upon a jaunt
of recreation and curiosity; and was invited, whilst there, to undertake a History of the War of Texan Independence, by more than twenty of the most
conspicuous actors in that war." Ashbel Smith approached Foote with the
idea for the book at least as early as March 1839. "It is due to the cause of Liberty that a true narrative of Texian Independence should be submitted to the
world," wrote Smith. "Appreciating your great literary attainments, your high
standing, the independence of your character and your devotion to the cause
of Liberty, we respectfully ask if . . . [you will] prepare for the world a History
of Texas." And Smith was by no means the only member of Lamar's circle
pressing for a written history to strengthen the administration's political position. In August, Thomas J. Green of Bexar County wrote that it must be
perfectly plain that the time had arrived when Lamar and his administration

required vindication "by responsible names. . . . I know the history of our young country full well and know too these acts only want telling by the *proper* persons and in the proper way. Upon this matter let me refer you more particularly to our friend General Foote with whom we have talked freely." Indeed, Lamar apparently was himself already acquainted and in correspondence with Foote. Between March 30 and April 27, 1839, Foote had addressed at least three letters of introduction to Lamar. Some sort of arrangement seems to have been made shortly thereafter, for in early June, Memucan Hunt, Texas representative on the joint United States–Texas boundary commission, made reference to meeting with Foote in Mississippi "previous to [Foote's] departure for Texas to compile its history."[15] By fall, Foote and Lamar had established regular correspondence concerning the progress of Foote's history. Lamar's influence was evident throughout, as manifested in Foote's attitude toward Sam Houston as well as Houston's attitude toward Foote. Foote portrayed William Travis, Branch T. Archer, and Ben Milam as heroes of epic proportions, while slyly criticizing Houston "in a spirit of *impartiality* . . . by stating the view entertained on either side in Texas" and by noting what the commander in chief of the Texans, had he been a truly great leader like Frederick of Prussia or Napoleon or Jackson, *might* have done. Houston, in return, referred to Foote's book in November 1841 as "*the Foot history*" because it would be "more footed than eyed."[16]

Foote made it clear from the outset that he viewed history as a tale of morality, Texas history being a prime example. He attributed the cause of the conflict between Mexico and Texas not to cultural differences but entirely to moral ones. According to Foote, it was the moral nature of the conflict that aroused so much interest and made Texas history so worthy a subject for study. "It is that *sublime collision of moral influences,* for the first time, now met in dread encounter, which has gathered, as it were, the generous-minded of all nations, around the outspread arena of conflict."[17]

Foote launched his narrative with remarks on the condition of Europe and Spain at the time of the Mexican conquest and moved rapidly to conclusions completely in keeping with prevailing romantic notions of heroes and villains. With bemusing irony, he described one portion of the territory "opened by the genius of Columbus to the enterprise of civilized colonists of the Old World" as the abode of *Science* and the *Arts,* "where, beneath the majestic banner of civil and religious freedom, the mind of man, disburdened of the shackles of prejudice, and redeemed from the paralyzing sway of bigotry, dares to assert its own *absolute independence,* acknowledging no authority save that of cultivated reason, and yielding no obedience save to the lessons of *truth.*" At the same time he charged that in another portion of that territory, "more ample in extent of territorial surface, and greatly more favoured by the bounty of Providence," human dignity had been "utterly prostrated, and the true ends of human exertion almost wholly disregarded; whilst *ignorance* and *vice,* and anarchical despotism have been permitted to wield the sceptre of a vile and debasing dominion over the most sacred rights and most precious privileges of humanity." This irony was heightened by the fact that Foote not only blithely overlooked the great moral stain of slavery while waving the "majestic banner of civil and religious freedom" but ten years later had to resign the governorship of Mississippi and flee to California because of his Unionist sympathies.[18]

The entire two-volume history lived up to the grandiosity of its introduction both in style and in its flagrant distortions of facts, which included justifications for the actions of Aaron Burr, James Wilkinson, and Haden Edwards, and condescending excuses for the implied cowardice of General Houston. "Those who commanded at Goliad and Bexar," Foote loftily asserted, "are not censurable for *anything.*" According to his version of the history of the war in Texas, *all* Texans were unblemished heroes and *all* Mexicans were "vulgar tyrants" and "demoniacal" agents, and their cohorts "unprincipled renegades." Although in discussing the conquest of Mexico, Foote alluded to the respected works of Gonzalo Fernández de Oviedo, Bernal Díaz, and Abbé D. Francesco Saverio Clavigero, as well as manuscript papers of Burr and Edwards, he obtained most of his information concerning the Texas Revolution and the history of the republic from personal interviews with participants.[19]

Henry Foote, like most of his predecessors, claimed that he had undertaken to write an *impartial* history of the war in Texas and repeatedly referred to his spirit of *impartiality* (emphasis Foote's), particularly preceding some of his most biased representations. In fact, although he was the first Texas historian in the nineteenth century to claim that his whole inspiration and purpose was moral edification, Foote was the first to be hired to write a history of Texas expressly for promoting the partisan views of a political administration. He was also the first to attempt deliberately to cover his real motives for writing. Editors of the *New York Review,* in comparing the works of Kennedy and Foote, had little to say regarding the latter, giving it a single, tactfully understated sentence. "We have not particularly adverted to the work of Mr. Foote, in the foregoing paper, as it is, in great measure, occupied with earlier historical details than have engaged our attention, and as, also, we wished, rather to present our readers with the impressions [of a traveler from abroad] than those which had been made . . . upon one of our own citizens, who might, perhaps, be supposed to have a stronger personal interest in speaking favorably of it."[20] Their remarks further revealed the edge foreign observers held over domestic writers in the esteem of United States editors.

Certainly, Foote's history contained all the requisite elements of romantic history. The themes of liberty, progress, and Providence were ever prominent. In moral tone and descriptive narrative he rivaled even the effusive Reverend Newell. Foote, however, went beyond either history or literature to produce a parody of both in form and substance. In so doing, he became the first, intentionally, to treat the whole subject of Texas history, and particularly modern history, as heroic myth.

A third book on Texas to appear in 1841 boasted considerably fewer pretensions than its contemporaries. Many of the differences between *Texas in 1840* and the works of Kennedy and Foote probably owed to the fact that it was written by a Calvinist preacher rather than by politicians. The Reverend A. B. Lawrence, a Presbyterian minister and editor of the *New Orleans Presbyterian,* visited Texas in 1839–40 and while there wrote a volume primarily intended as an immigrant guide but later published as *A History of Texas.*[21]

Lawrence, like Foote, found in Texas history a great moral lesson but with considerably more sincerity. Where for Foote the moral aspect had been merely a front for his real purpose of deliberate political propaganda, for Lawrence the purpose of history was to provide fodder for a sermon, and he determined to make the most of Texas history. Lawrence's work illustrated the prevalent idea that for people to fully understand or appreciate a description of a place, they must have a knowledge of its history, and, conversely, in order to understand or appreciate the history of a place, readers must possess information about its geography and culture. In his preface, Lawrence professed a desire to furnish useful information to the thousands "flocking towards the new and rising star of the west," and to aid that country in "gaining to herself an industrious, intelligent, and virtuous population." In the process, Lawrence, either consciously or unconsciously, constructed a case for the annexation of Texas by the United States.[22]

By all accounts, including his own, Lawrence intended his first publication, *Texas in 1840, Or the Emigrant's Guide to the New Republic,* to be just that.[23] He devoted 200 of the book's 275 pages to chapters on agriculture, geology, flora and fauna, ornithology and entomology, cities and towns, and society and manners. In addition, he included his diary of his tour from Galveston to Austin. It is also clear from his introduction to the book that he considered it an opportunity to point out the instructiveness of history. What the history of Texas taught, Lawrence maintained, was the triumph of right principles over wrong. Like Chester Newell and Henry S. Foote, Lawrence adopted an unqualified pro-Texas stance. The causes of the Texan Revolution, he asserted, differed "essentially from the causes of all other similar events, with the single exception of that which produced the independence of the United States. . . . High principles of religious and political freedom, ardent patriotism, generous devotedness to the cause of regulated liberty and lofty heroism marked the character of the leaders in the great struggle of Texian independence." As Lawrence warmed to his subject, he broadened the implications of the war in Texas to embrace the history of the Protestant Reformation and freeing the world from the tyranny of the Catholic Church, which he equated with the empire of Satan. Thus, he eagerly furthered the maturing romantic American westering myth that had Providence proclaiming manifest destiny: "Mexico herself will in the event appear to be but a suburb of the extended territory to be pervaded by the conquering power of the gospel of Jesus. Guatemala and all South America will feel the bland influence of the light of the Sun of Righteousness rising." In this missionary context, Lawrence viewed the history and relations of Texas as nothing less than the "beginning of the downfall of Antichrist."[24]

Despite his professed intention to immigrate permanently to Texas, Reverend Lawrence never actually did so. His original publication, *Texas in 1840,* was reprinted in 1842, with the year updated, and in 1844 and 1845 with the title changed to *A History of Texas.* Referred to by bibliographer John H. Jenkins as "scissors and paste" history, his work well illustrated the haziness that surrounded the definition and purpose of written history in America during the first half of the nineteenth century, and it illuminated the growing tendency to transform romantic themes into efficacious myths. America was growing. If right principles were to triumph, they must remain consistent with that growth. As discrepancies began to appear between those traditional principles and the realities of a growing nation, the need for myths to correct them increased apace.

An antidote to the promotional histories of the Lamar administration, specifically to William Kennedy's work, appeared almost reflexively in 1842 with *The History of the Republic of Texas, from the Discovery of the Country to the Present Time; and the Cause of Her Separation from the Republic of Mexico,* by Nicholas Doran P. Maillard, a bitterly frustrated British investor in Mexican bonds. Actually, this book had more in common with Foote's blatant propaganda than with Kennedy's. In contrast to Kennedy's book, which though undeniably pro-Texan was impeccably researched and faithfully written, Maillard's work graphically demonstrated the ruthlessness with which "history" might be used to selfish and material ends. Jenkins accurately called it "the most vitriolic denunciation of the Republic of Texas, written with absolutely no regard for the truth."[25]

Maillard arrived in Texas in early 1840, representing to local residents of Richmond, Fort Bend County, where he took up residence, that he had been lured to Texas by its genial climate and glorious history, that he had been a barrister in London and a literary man, and that he intended to buy a plantation, settle down, practice law, and write a book.[26] In the introduction to his book, Maillard claimed that, in delicate health, he had been seduced into coming to Texas by "exaggerated accounts then, as well as now, promulgated respecting Texas and the Texans." He did gain admission to the Texas bar in April 1840, became coeditor of the Richmond *Telescope,* and gained a local reputation as a master bartender. According to Fort Bend County historian Clarence R. Wharton's sources, he also burned a great deal of midnight oil writing a novel or taking notes on the law, depending on whom one asked. Also according to local accounts, Maillard spent a great deal of time in the company of one James Riddell, a gunsmith and cutler in Richmond, leading to speculation that the two had known each other elsewhere. Maillard's subsequent admission to being a Mexican bondholder increased suspicion that Riddell had been a spy for the same bondholders committee.[27]

While living in Richmond, Maillard made several trips to Houston and one to Austin. He returned to London in late summer or early fall of 1840. Wharton suggested that Maillard's original plan had been to gather material and write a series of articles for publication that would turn public opinion in England against Texas, at least sufficiently to cause the Palmerston ministry to require Texas to accept land warrants issued by Mexico in 1839 to English bondholders in lieu of payment on Mexican bonds. Once back in England, Maillard decided to write a legal brief instead, which could be used in a discussion of the Mexican bond question in Parliament, and later expanded it into a history.[28] His book appeared in early 1842. Despite the expressions of disgust and outrage from both contemporary and later critics over Maillard's gross misrepresentations and defamation of Texas, he claimed to be objective and impartial. He began by informing his readers that his object was "to present to the public an unvarnished account of what Texas and the Texans really [were]." Yet, in the same breath he issued far-from-objective judgments "of the true origin and history of their rebellion against Mexico, their lawful sovereign; of their inhuman treatment of the Negro and Indian races; of their aggressive policy systematically pursued toward Mexico." He admitted further that his purpose was to prevent England or Englishmen from entering into a treaty with Texas. Maillard insisted that Mexico would have been a more lucrative trading partner, that the dividends of such a relationship with Mexico would have been remitted on the English debt, and that a large part of that debt could have been canceled by the lands in Texas pledged by Mexico to the bondholders. He conveniently failed to acknowledge that the lands were pledged by Mexico in 1837, *after* San Jacinto, and therefore disputable from the outset.[29]

Ironically, in view of what was known or suspected about his activities in Texas, Maillard's criticism of Kennedy provided a classic example of the "pot calling the kettle black." Admitting Kennedy's work was "obviously got up with great care" and of "considerable merit" in language and composition, he continued: "The historian should be more careful of his facts than of his language; these are to be collected by careful observation, and not imbibed while sipping champagne and inhaling the crafty inspiration of astute young Yankee lawyers congregated in Texas, first, to seize the country; secondly, to turn its resources to their own profit; and thirdly, to justify the act."[30] Although Maillard's estimation of Texan motives may not have been entirely off the mark, his own *History* was in fact filled with errors, large and small, such as dating the Adams-Onís Treaty in 1829, which he attempted to excuse as owing to "distressing illness in [his] family, and other pressing incidents." His presentation of the information he accumulated in his visit to Texas more nearly resembled the novel he was rumored to be writing than nonfiction. By contemporary standards, it succeeded as neither. Although he included excerpts or full texts from many historical documents, Maillard could never have been mistaken for "objective and impartial" by even the most sympathetic critic. "Maillard's *History of Texas*," wrote one English reviewer, "is as wholly anti-Texan as it is possible for any man, even for Mr. Kennedy, to be thoroughly on the opposing side. But the one-sidedness of the author before us may be more easily accounted for, according to his own showing, than the partiality evinced by the other writer."[31] As history, his work offered no moral instruction or even entertainment. It had no literary qualities that might distinguish it as art. Easily verifiable mistakes were so numerous as to render its execution sloppy and its "truths" or insights suspect, even when there was some truth to them. Unfortunately for him, in his palpable "hatred of the land of promise," Maillard was hoist with his own petard. His *History* succeeded neither as history nor as propaganda since it apparently had no appreciable effect on British recognition of Texas independence, which was finally completed in June 1842. "A book has also lately issued from the press under the auspices of the Mexican and Colonial interests attacking Texas and the Texians in a manner the most false and virulent," wrote Arthur Ikin, British consul for the Republic of Texas, to Anson Jones. "Notwithstanding all this attack, the country is become better known and appreciated among commercial men." Ashbel Smith confirmed Ikin's conclusion: "In the interest of the persons hostile to our country a book styled a History of Texas has been published, characterized by a most extraordinary disregard for decency and of truth. J. Doran Maillard is the avowed author. He addressed a letter to Lord Aberdeen of the date of Sept. 24th, 1841, in the nature of a caution and remonstrance against the acknowledgement of our independence, etc. . . . I do not perceive however, that Maillard's letter produced the slightest effect in this quarter."[32]

Promotion of Texan interests in the 1840s came from more than one camp. While Lamar, Burnet, and their supporters sought to strengthen Texas' position as an independent nation, others, both in Texas and the United States, continued to pursue annexation. Those who wished to advance or deter such interests also turned to history as a vehicle for promoting their respective views. One who had long entertained an interest in Spanish America and its relationship to the United States was John M. Niles of Connecticut. Niles published *A View of South America and Mexico* in 1825. As a United States senator from 1835 to 1839, he gained a reputation for being disturbingly nonpartisan, refusing to vote immediately for the recognition of Texas, much to the chagrin of fellow Democrats. During his second term, 1843–49, he was even less partisan. He turned distinctly protectionist and expressed little support for the Mexican War. In 1844, as the debate over Texas raged, he republished his book on South America and Mexico as a history, this time including a short history of Texas. "Lying, as Texas does, upon our borders . . . it cannot fail to be an object of intense interest," he wrote, making it irresistible by describing it, as had others, as the "garden of the earth."[33] Niles assured his readers that this history was authoritative since someone "on the spot" had supplied the facts.

The contributor of this historical view of Texas, Lorrain Thompson Pease, did indeed have information from someone on the spot. Also from Connecticut and connected by marriage to Niles, Pease was the father of Elisha Marshall Pease, future governor of Texas, who had settled there in 1835 and was presumably his father's chief source of information. Whether L. T. Pease ever actually visited Texas himself is unclear. His brief history comprised 126 pages of Niles's first volume and contained little that was "fresh" despite the editor's claim. His themes—liberty, patriotism, progress of the Anglo-American race—reflected typically romantic assumptions of his day, as did his style, though even that lacked the vividness of imagery considered by many to be essential in writing history. In the first chapter, Pease set the scene for his historical narrative by describing the boundaries, geography, soil, climate, waterways, transportation, towns, and inhabitants, touting the region as the realization of "dreams of a paradise on earth." He dismissed Texas history prior to the establishment of Austin's colony as "little more than the history of the wandering tribes of savages" who had roamed the wilderness for "countless ages." Indeed, according to Pease, the early history of the country was so unimportant as to be unknown prior to the signing of the Onís Treaty in 1819. To the early "adventurous spirits" from the United States he attributed the influence that enabled the natives to "throw off the Spanish yoke." In other words, Pease asserted, Texas had no history prior to Anglo-American influence, and thus, by implication, its history was part and parcel of United States history. He presented the Texans as brave and self-sacrificing buffers between the forces of good and evil.[34]

Pease's account continued through the victory of San Jacinto, which he portrayed as a victory of global significance. He uncovered no new sources and made slight use of traditional ones such as Austin's 1836 Louisville address, military records, government documents, and personal accounts of participants, "men of unquestioned veracity." In none of these sources did Pease find cause for closer scrutiny because analysis was not his goal. The truth he already knew. His history was not intended to judge it but merely to prove it, a fact that became evident with his concluding plea for the annexation of Texas to the United States, the only prudent thing for both sides.[35]

Other publications in the early 1840s, such as that of Arthur Ikin, an Englishman with an interest in Texas lands who was appointed Texan consul to Great Britain in 1841, and Mathilda Houstoun, wife of a British army officer who visited Texas in late 1842, portrayed Texas and Texans in an equally favorable light. Ikin's work, intended to encourage immigration, was purely promotional literature. Houstoun, already well known in British literary circles, wrote a witty and insightful account of her observations of Texas and Texans as she encountered them while visiting with her husband, undoubtedly to amuse herself and to satisfy the curiosity of her compatriots. An equally candid but less sanguine guidebook by the founder of New Braunfels appeared in 1846.[36] All were primarily concerned with Texas and Texans as they were, and any references to their history was incidental to that aim.

In addition to these, a number of personal narratives appeared recounting the adventures of their authors in various Texas scrapes. The earliest to appear were the memoirs of Hermann Ehrenberg, a German immigrant and member of the New Orleans Greys, who fought in the Texas Revolution. Ehrenberg's memoirs consisted of a colorful review of his adventures as a soldier. This effort was followed in annual succession by accounts of participants in the Santa Fe and Mier expeditions. Although they made great reading, they were first and foremost frontier adventure stories.[37]

The fate of the Texas republic produced a flurry of publications in the first half of the decade that faded markedly with the final passage of Texas statehood in 1845–46, and a Mexican history of the Texas Revolution had yet to be written. However, with the Treaty of Guadalupe Hidalgo making the loss of Texas forever a reality, the first history of Texas and its revolution by a Mexican appeared. Its author, General Vicente Filisola, Santa Anna's second in command, had published a defense of the Texas campaign as early as 1836.[38] More than simply a defense of conduct or the personal memoirs of an event, Filisola's *Memorias para la Historia de la Guerra de Tejas,* published in September 1848, brought the entire history of Texas colonization to bear on the Texas Revolution and its outcome. Its composition reflected not only personal observations but references to earlier histories and important original documents written in Texas.

Vicente Filisola, a native of Italy, wrote from the perspective of a professional soldier who had served both for and against the Mexican army. He had joined the Spanish army at an early age and participated in the Napoleonic Wars before being sent to Mexico, where he continued to serve the Royalist army until 1821 when he became an officer of the Mexican army under Iturbide. He had himself received a colonization grant in Texas in 1831 and from 1833 had been charged with stemming the flow of American immigration into Texas. According to his editors, he had been working on his memoirs for a number of years, but since the publication of Maillard's history in 1842, he had been particularly pressured by the desire to "confront it with another history from the pen of a Mexican."[39]

The editors of this work assured their readers that they would find in it "the truth of the matter set straight and made manifest" by "the most important and impartial information." Their only goal, they insisted, was the objective truth. They were convinced that knowing the history of Texas would enable present and future generations to benefit from the faults and errors that led to the loss of Texas and the potential compromise of Mexico's independence and national existence. At the same time, both Filisola and his editors recognized the difficulty in writing objective contemporary history.[40]

Filisola began his history with a brief review of the claim that Spain, and later Mexico, had upon Texas in order to conclude that the United States had no legitimate claim to Texas based upon the Louisiana Purchase. He maintained, as had some earlier Texas historians, that from 1803 onward the United States had, nevertheless, cast an avaricious eye in that direction and that those North Americans who ventured into Texas, whatever their pretext, were motivated solely by greed. That they were able to do so Filisola attributed to the abandonment of the mission/presidio system. Thus, with considerable honesty, he pointed out the errors and shortcomings of both Spain and the United States. He credited Spain, however, with making a well-intentioned effort to correct its mistakes by undertaking a project to build the population of Texas, an effort that failed because it was interrupted by the break between Great Britain and Spain and by the abortive revolution led by Miguel Hidalgo.[41]

Filisola exhibited an ability to assess events of Texas history honestly on various occasions. In his accounts of military engagements he excelled, being able to give a particularly balanced evaluation no doubt because, as a professional soldier, he understood them thoroughly. He astutely placed blame for the murders of Manuel de Salcedo and Simón de Herrera on Bernardo Gutiérrez, taking note of the resistance of the North Americans and other foreigners serving with Gutiérrez's troops to the proceedings. He asserted that Moses Austin, being down on his luck, was out to grab the main chance with his plan to become a colonizer of Texas under the conditions of the Spanish government, but he credited Stephen F. Austin for his fortitude in facing the trials of maintaining the colony against nature and marauding Indians.[42]

In fact, in his assessment of Austin, Filisola revealed the differences in worldview that separated the Mexican understanding of Texas history from that of North Americans and Europeans. In his view, Austin occupied the catbird seat, poised to become the most powerful citizen not only in Texas but in the whole Mexican republic. Filisola confessed his utter mystification that Austin would then sacrifice all "the fruits of his anxieties and sufferings" to an adherence to "theories of independence and exaggerated liberty for himself and his people." In a flash of insight, Filisola noted that Austin's dreams were "in truth snatched from him later by the new wave of adventurers and criminals who came in . . . and these people took over his lands."[43] Though, like other historians of the romantic era, he interpreted the hand of Providence in the course of events, Filisola made it plain that his basic assumptions about morality and history were not the same as those of American romantics. For Filisola, duty and obedience (values important to a soldier) rather than liberty were paramount. He could not understand why the Texas colonists did not just obey the law, whatever it was. That, as he saw it, was the duty of a citizen. Anglo-Americans believed if they opposed the government, they should revolt. That, as they saw it, was their right as citizens.

Ultimately, Filisola concluded that, whatever the immorality or culpability of the North Americans, the loss of Texas was the result of Mexico's own mistakes and inexperience. "Our blindness has been such that we have *given away* the lands of a paradise, we have granted them without stipend or any sort of advantage to our enemies. . . . right now we are receiving the punishment that our lack of foresight has deserved." The purpose of his history was to help Mexico learn from its mistakes, to profit by the lessons of history, and, as far as Filisola was concerned, they were not moral lessons but practical ones.[44]

The Mexican War and its aftermath produced a spate of war memoirs, travel accounts, immigrant guides, and a natural history. The first personal account of the Mexican War appeared in 1846. Another followed in 1847. These anecdotal volumes provided valuable eyewitness accounts but did not dwell on the history of the conflict. One of the best immigrant guides yet issued appeared as the decade drew to a close. Its author, Viktor Bracht, came to Texas as an emissary of the German government for the purpose of assisting in colonization activities. His book, *Texas Im Jahre 1848* (Texas in 1848), provided a thorough critical study of the country, its flora, fauna, and people. Bracht was forthright in both praise and criticism. Nevertheless, he wrote purely to provide useful, up-to-date information specifically for the German immigrant and did not dwell on the past, either distant or recent.[45]

In the 1840s, the volume of publications on Texas increased along with its population. The issues of boundary, Anglo-American settlement, and independence had produced intense interest in Texas during the 1830s. Foreign and domestic issues related to American expansion, as well as the availability of so much free land for immigrants, produced even greater interest during the 1840s. Another half-dozen histories appeared, mostly as utilitarian as those of the 1830s had been, with a few subtle differences. Whereas the historians of the 1830s had written for personal gain of one kind or another, historians of Texas in the 1840s were, for the most part, motivated less by self-interest than by promotion of some larger cause. Only one, Maillard, wrote primarily to further personal interests. Although they all professed impartiality, on the whole they produced a decidedly more pro-Texan view of Texas history than their predecessors had done a decade earlier, as well as a more distinctly racial and moralistic one. They obviously viewed the relationship of past to present as one of cause and effect, whose chief value was to teach moral lessons, the most important being that right principles triumphed. The Texans had won; their cause must have been right.

The Texas historians of the 1840s referred frequently to romantic themes of morality, patriotism, progress, and Providence and emphasized them vigorously with respect to the general topic of Anglo-American expansion. As previous writers had done, they perpetuated the westering myth of the frontier Eden, but they also expanded on it, incorporating, more emphatically than ever before, the right of those who cultivated the land to possess it, an addition necessary to the moral acceptability of aggressive territorial expansion: America's manifest destiny. These writers had access to more documentation than had ever been available before. Although some of them used sources lightly with little evaluation and few footnotes, others documented thoughtfully and thoroughly, resulting in some of the best and worst scholarship on Texas to date. Like other works written in the romantic period, their accounts of battles and other emotionally charged events tended toward the dramatic, though only Foote engaged in much embellishment and romantic ornamentation.

In background and occupation, writers of Texas history during the 1840s fitted the profile of the romantic historian. All were well-educated professionals: writers, editors, preachers, lawyers, politicians, diplomats, and soldiers. Few, if any, wrote with the expectation of deriving much gain directly from book sales. They differed, however, from the greatly admired and imitated patrician models of romantic history—Prescott, Motley, Bancroft, and Parkman—in that none of them set out to write a definitive history. They all had some primary agenda and used history not as an end in itself but as a means to achieve particular ends. At the middle of the nineteenth century, Texas had become a state and the center of raging controversy. Texas history had become romantic because romance enhanced its utility.

4 ★ Pride Goeth . . . before a Fall

History Writing in Antebellum Texas

The Treaty of Guadalupe Hidalgo not only ended the dispute with Mexico over the boundary of Texas but institutionalized Anglo-American hegemony to the Pacific coast of North America. The addition of so much territory provided fuel for the already-hot fires of sectionalism in the United States. In the third quarter of the nineteenth century, national turmoil and divided loyalties would leave the new state of Texas grappling for its sense of identity. At the same time, the events of that turbulent quarter century inevitably brought changes in the approach to history writing generally and in the basic assumptions that had shaped it for more than fifty years. These changes began to appear in the writing of Texas historians by the 1850s.

For the first half of the nineteenth century, historians shared with their audience basic assumptions about essence, morality, progress, and national character. When people began to disagree on these points, a different approach to historical scholarship and a different kind of history began to develop.[1] In the second half of the nineteenth century, the study of history developed as a discipline, distinct from literature, and emphasis shifted from the general to the particular. Sectional differences in the United States soon proved to be intellectual as well as economic and geographic. The Romantic Movement that swept America between 1815 and 1861 evolved differently in different sections of the country. Romantic themes were reflected in various humanitarian movements in New England and in religious revival meetings on the Western frontier. Southern romanticism was colored more by local considerations than in other sections. The result was a distinctive and influential force that some historians of the South have argued contributed substantially to the creation of a strong sense of Southern nationalism by 1860.[2]

Perhaps the first indication of the shift in interest from general to particular in Texas history appeared in William Gouge's *Fiscal History of Texas* in
1852. Instead of attempting a comprehensive treatment as had earlier writers,
Gouge limited his topic to the financial history of the Texas Revolution and
of the Republic of Texas. Gouge, a native of Philadelphia, had a reputation
for his opposition to banks, corporations, and paper money. Nevertheless, he
spent his life engaged in banking and finance. He had been editor of the
Philadelphia *Gazette* and *The Journal of Banking* and had authored several
books on finance from a historical perspective before turning his attention to
Texas. Following a visit to Texas in 1852, he became a special agent of the
United States Treasury Department, served as accountant for the State Bank
of Arkansas, and wrote the *Report of the Accountants of the State Bank of Arkansas* in 1858. Gouge's bias against national banks was evident, and he was
severely criticized by Texans like Sam Houston, who accused him of writing
specifically for the purpose of sabotaging Texas' credit reputation, but he had
to be considered knowledgeable about his subject. Moreover, biographical
sources have suggested that his biased attitude had mellowed by the time he
arrived in Texas.[3]

Gouge readily admitted a specific purpose for writing a financial history
of the Texas republic that extended beyond the desire to give a simple objective account of what happened. Over the course of his life, he had arrived at conclusions about the American system of public credit and the
dangers of paper currency that he believed had to be demonstrated to the
American people. As to why he chose to write such a particular history, he
explained, "History is of importance only as it illustrates principles; and
principles may be as strikingly illustrated in the small communities of
Rhode Island, Delaware, or Texas, as in the larger ones of New York, Massachusetts, or Virginia." He chose Texas for much the same reasons as earlier historians had. "In the short period of seven months," he observed,
"[the Texans] achieved the independence of a country larger than Great
Britain and Ireland, and for ten years, without direct aid from any foreign
government, they sustained this independence, in defiance of all the attempts which a nation of ten millions made to reduce them to subjection.
The history of such a people cannot be without interest." Furthermore,
Gouge observed that if the proper history should be of classical proportions, Texas qualified as well as any subject. "As we proceed," he assured
readers, "it will be found that all the fiscal faults which the great nations of
Europe and America have committed on a large scale, the Texans have
committed on a small."[4]

Gouge also intended that his history, though narrative, be scientific with regard to the accumulation and use of sources: "The extracts . . . are given in distinct type. This gives the volume all the advantages of a documentary history." Likewise, he made it plain that his was not to be a picturesque, imaginative history designed to captivate a wide audience. "If the book is not as amusing as the last new novel, the writer cannot help it. . . . He does not write for boarding-school misses. . . . Some of the details may be interesting to few but citizens of Texas, and creditors of Texas; but the principles involved are highly important, not only to those whose political position requires them to study finance as a science, but to all who are in any way interested in the preservation of the public faith when pledged for the payment of public debts." Thus, admitted Gouge, history provided him means to an end, a view expressed earlier the same year by the *North American Review* in arguing that historical investigation might be immediately useful even if the broader implications of the knowledge gathered might not be discernible for generations: "The means are nominally considered inferior in dignity and importance to the end which they are made to subserve; but the end may be a distant, even an unattainable one, while the use of the means is immediately and constantly productive of good."[5]

Although Gouge did not write to amuse or entertain and freely admitted the dryness of his materials, he did not lack for a sense of humor, albeit as dry as his subject. As a result, he undoubtedly amused himself and his more perspicacious readers with his frequently tongue-in-cheek style. Nowhere is this better illustrated than in his analysis of the failure of General James Hamilton's negotiation of a loan for the republic in 1841 and its application to the principle, by then gaining in popularity, that the smallest detail of human relations might have the profoundest effect on society. At the same time he derided any tendency the Texans might have to take themselves too seriously. Gouge recounted how, threatened with another invasion by Mexico and without funds to provide for Texas' defense, President Lamar struck upon the idea of negotiating a loan for the republic with the Bank of Messrs. J. Lafitte & Co., to be guaranteed by the French government. The negotiations appeared to be proceeding nicely, Gouge told his readers, until difficulties arose between the French minister to Texas and an Austin tavern keeper by the name of Bullock, whose pigs had trespassed on the property of M. de Saligny, whereupon they were killed by the Frenchman's servant. Mr. Bullock, in turn, whipped the servant, thereby enraging Saligny, who sought justice by influencing his brother-in-law, as luck would have it, the French minister of finance at Paris. Consequently, Hamilton's loan was defeated. With all seriousness, Gouge explained the providential implications of this controversy:

All Texas stood by Mr. Bullock and his pigs. Houstonites and Anti-Houstonites were of one accord. Nor will it be too much to say that, as Rome was saved by the cackling of geese, so Texas was saved by the squeaking of pigs. If the loan had been obtained, it would have been used in establishing a national bank, by which every dollar would have been made to look like ten. The result would have been that the debt of Texas, instead of being twelve millions, would have been twenty-five, thirty, perhaps forty millions. The most intelligent Texans agree in opinion that this would have been the result. All honor, then, to Mr. Bullock and his pigs; and this heretofore much despised animal must be regarded hereafter as possessed of classic interest. If his figure, carved in marble, should be placed over the entrance of the treasury of Texas, it would serve as a memento to future ages of his having been the salvation of the republic, and teach Mr. Branch Tanner Archer's "thousands and millions, born and unborn," that the humblest of agents may be instrumental in producing consequences of the utmost importance.[6]

Texans reacted defensively to Gouge's book when it appeared and were bitterly critical of what they considered his bizarre fiscal views long afterward. Half a century later, historian George P. Garrison condemned it for its "tone of rasping criticism." Outside Texas, however, critics received the work more charitably and dispassionately. "The historian has not only presented all the facts bearing on the debts of Texas in the order of their occurrence in a very clear and striking manner," wrote a reviewer for *DeBow's,* "but has made his narrative a vehicle for enforcing sound doctrines on subjects of the highest importance to the public at all times—such as the nature of state securities, the obligation imposed by public debts, together with numerous questions concerning currency and finance, which are far more clearly and forcibly illustrated by the progress and result of the measure explained in the history, than could be done by any didactic statements." Moreover, these critics recognized in Gouge's work the operation of general laws: "The book is, in fact, a book of political philosophy, in which the conduct of Texas is taken as the theme, and the true principles of currency and finance thereby illustrated, for the most part, by 'the rule of opposites.'"[7]

Gouge's book was, if nothing else, representative of its time: transitional. A blend of anecdotal, narrative, and documentary history, it focused on one aspect of human activity in microcosm rather than attempting a full sweep. It was considered unacceptably biased by those with opposing biases—that is, Texans sensitive to any criticism of their national character and supporters of Nicholas Biddle and national banks. Yet, as John H. Jenkins has pointed out, it was no more biased than other early-nineteenth-century Texas history, and it brought to light an aspect not previously examined in any depth. It was not written for the general reader but for a limited audience, who might, if willing, heed the warning that the historian interpreted as the operation of general laws evidenced in history.[8]

In the year after the publication of Gouge's *Fiscal History of Texas,* another author with a limited focus began to publish his commentaries on a previously neglected aspect of the history of Texas. José Antonio Navarro, a signer of the Texas Declaration of Independence and one of the republic's most influential founding fathers, began publishing a series of historical commentaries designed primarily to write the ignored and diminished historical contributions of Tejanos into the history of their state. Although Navarro had long been a Tejano advocate, he acted specifically in response to Anglo-American renderings of Tejano history in the early 1850s, such as Francis Baylies's *A Campaign in Mexico, in the Years 1846, 1847 & 1848,* and articles in local newspapers, the San Antonio *Western Texan* (October 14, 1852), and the *San Antonio Ledger* (September 15, 1853), all of which portrayed the Tejano population as morally and intellectually impoverished and dependent on the Anglo-American influence for redemption of their heritage. Through a series of commentaries or historical chronicles published in English in the local press between 1853 and 1857, Navarro intended to set the record straight concerning the history of the people who developed San Antonio and sacrificed their lives for it. He also had a more immediate and political purpose, that of discouraging Americans "who with base and aggressive pretexts" wanted to displace legitimate citizens who were descendants of these people. He attempted to do so by drawing parallels between Anglo-Texans and the revolutionary struggles of the Tejanos of San Antonio, who were "guided only by an instinct for their liberty, against enemies so superior that they may be placed alongside the most free and fortunate nations of all mankind—such as the nation with the flag of stars." Like Gouge, Navarro did not write for a wide audience but for a specific one. Initially, he translated his comments into English for publication because he wrote for an Anglo-American audience, and he appealed specifically to a smaller segment of that readership: "I do not write for the heartless nor for the egoists—to whom the glories and misfortunes of men of another origin and language matter little or not at all. I write for the humanitarian and cultured who understand how to respect and empathize with the tribulations of a valiant people."[9]

Navarro's chief authority about the facts was his own eyewitness account, but he referred to manuscript sources, such as Bernardo Gutiérrez's written account of the infamous executions of Governors Manuel de Salcedo, Simón de Herrera, and company, in order to support his recollections and his rendering of events that he did not witness firsthand. His comments centered mainly on the struggle for Mexican independence, commencing with Miguel Hidalgo y Costilla, and were limited to the defense of San Antonio de Bexar. "This is an imperfect but truthful history of the events of that period," he wrote. "You will not discover vainglory, nor the inordinate desire for excellence of style," he warned, "but rather a concise narrative of bloody and revolutionary times." Navarro readily admitted that he had no aspirations as a literary historian: "I write this booklet as an inveterate devotee to historical materials, without literary pretensions, against all mercenary purposes, and feeling myself free and above those who do such for profit."[10] If his style, method, biases, and use of history did not particularly distinguish him, Navarro was distinctive as a Texas historian in the nineteenth century in other respects. He was the first to write a series of historical articles rather than a monograph, undoubtedly with the intention of assuring they would thus most likely be read. Not only were his commentaries the first Tejano publication on Texas history, but Navarro himself was the first aspiring Texas historian born on Texas soil and a lifelong citizen of that country.

Not all antebellum histories of Texas dealt with such limited topics. At least one historian of the era produced a comprehensive history of Texas that would have a lasting impact. In the preface to his *Fiscal History of Texas* in 1852, William Gouge had bemoaned the want of "a good general history of Texas ... that [the history] by Kennedy extending no further than to 1839–1840." By the time Henderson Yoakum published his *History of Texas* in 1855, the clamor in Texas for a general history of the state had reached a crescendo, and in his work Texas not only achieved a definitive history but also reached the pinnacle of romantic nationalism. Yoakum, though he had never published a word before his *History of Texas* and never published another word after, became *the historian* of Texas, first and, in the minds of many, last. After his death in 1857, he was remembered in the Huntsville, Texas, *Bar and Bench* as "the father of Texas History. He did lay in the wilderness the foundation for a vigorous quest for truth." During his lifetime, Yoakum had been a soldier, a politician, a lawyer, an adviser, an amateur scientist, and a dedicated promoter of higher education, but when the Texas Centennial Committee erected a marker before his home in 1936, it was for his *History of Texas* that he was memorialized.[11]

Henderson Yoakum, as far as anyone knows, did not write his *History* for profit. Nevertheless, William Gouge was not the only one of the opinion that Texas needed a comprehensive history, and leading Texans, among them Yoakum's friend Judge P. W. Gray, had expressed their desire to see one published. Although Yoakum may have determined on his own initiative to write a history of his adopted state, he would have known such a work was impatiently awaited.

Yoakum's *History of Texas,* from the time of its publication, was one of the most highly regarded of all the state histories written during the antebellum era, and it has endured much longer than most, if not all, of them. It was also very much a product of its times: laboriously researched and documented, and thoroughly romantic. Touted for its objectivity, it was as biased as any of its predecessors. Herbert H. Lang, in what is probably the most exhaustive study of Yoakum, attributed Yoakum's success as a historian to the fact that he had "the zeal of a convert to a new cause for his subject." Others, however, have pointed out that it was not the zeal of a convert to a new cause but the zeal of an ideologue for an old one that inspired the pen of Henderson Yoakum.[12]

The key to Yoakum's approach to his *History of Texas* can be traced to his political career in his native state of Tennessee. He was an ardent admirer of Thomas Jefferson and a staunch supporter of Andrew Jackson, ideologically dedicated to agrarian republicanism and imperial expansion of the Union. He had been active in local Democratic politics during the 1830s. In 1836, he served as captain of the Murfreesboro Sentinels, a cavalry unit organized to aid the Texans in their war for independence, though the victory at San Jacinto precluded the need for the Tennesseans' help. Yoakum then enlisted for service on the Sabine frontier under General Edmund P. Gaines, and in 1838 he enlisted in the Tennessee infantry during an outbreak of hostilities between the army and the Cherokees. These military excursions reflected his political philosophy. Along with endorsement of Indian removal, he supported Democratic economic policies of "hard" money and an independent treasury. In a letter to Martin Van Buren in 1845, he asserted that the Western land belonged to the American agrarian because God planned for democrats like himself to displace the "savage" and enrich the land.[13]

Yoakum found both his ideology and his career threatened in the late 1830s and early 1840s by economic depression, which left his middle-Tennessee constituency more amenable to Whig ideas of industrialization and centralization. Like many other Jacksonians, Yoakum feared the changes that modern institutions were bringing. With his political career in shambles, he began casting about for a place to reconstruct his dream of an ideal republic, and the annexation of Texas provided just such an opportunity, a new republic in need of securing. In June 1845, he wrote Martin Van Buren that Texas was "the Italy of our continent," a place where "they hail the approach of that period when they can claim the eagle as their own." He told Van Buren that he believed Americans should pursue an aggressive policy in the West, replacing the "savages" and despotic Mexicans with "enterprising, industrious, thrifty" democrats because that was the only way Americans could "accomplish the great ends" of God.[14] In this frame of mind, Yoakum began his life in Texas as an attorney whose most prominent client and neighbor was another Jacksonian, Sam Houston.

Yoakum brought his democratic ideology to the writing of his *History of Texas*. If he wished to be thorough, accurate, and comprehensive in the collection and interpretation of the facts, he also wished to instruct his readers in the principles of virtue, patriotism, and morality. Although he acknowledged the need for more in-depth study of Texas' colonial past, Yoakum, like other European and American writers, regarded the period prior to Anglo-American settlement as the dark ages of Texas history, when "ignorance and despotism . . . hung like a dark cloud over [Texas'] noble forests and luxuriant pastures." The spirit of liberty loosed by the American Revolution, he argued, dispelled the dark cloud. According to Yoakum, the struggle between the forces of freedom and despotism, personified by Texas and Mexico, resulted in overwhelming victory for the forces of freedom at San Jacinto that was "physically and morally complete," for even "Providence seemed in every way to favor the result."[15]

Yoakum's style, though unquestionably romantic, evinced restraint. He avoided excessive ornamentation and exaggerated language, and he used anecdotes and figures of speech with discretion. Nevertheless, he succumbed to many of the habits of the romantic historians, such as improving upon the accuracy of impression of direct quotes when he believed his alterations came closer to the speaker's true intention. He defended his editorial attempt to improve upon the manuscript copy of Ellis P. Bean's memoirs by arguing that Bean "was but poorly educated, and his long residence in Mexico had caused him almost to forget his own language. Hence, it has become necessary to correct his manuscript and to rewrite it." On the other hand, much of Yoakum's enduring credibility derived from the apparent accuracy of his summaries and his faithfulness to the accounts he summarized.[16]

In choice and treatment of his subject, Henderson Yoakum also demonstrated himself to be a thoroughgoing romantic. He devoted nine pages to a colorful, detailed account of one minor skirmish between James Bowie and a roving band of Indians but only nine chapters to all of Texas history prior to the beginning of the Anglo-American period. Herbert Lang described this imbalance as Yoakum's "lack of a proper sense of proportion."[17] In fairness to Yoakum, events in Texas prior to Philip Nolan's excursions had been largely glossed over by everyone except Morfi and Pichardo, not only because there was lack of interest but because sources from that period were not easily accessible.

If Yoakum indulged in the dramatic appeal of hand-to-hand combat, he revealed his ideological leanings even more clearly in his heroes. Although he has often been criticized for his favoritism to Houston (most frequently by Houston's foes), his real hero was Stephen F. Austin, the pioneer and builder who overcame the wilderness in order to establish an empire on revolutionary principles of freedom and independence. "If he who, by conquest, wins an empire, and receives the world's applause, how much more is due to those who, by unceasing toil, lay in the wilderness the foundation for an infant colony, and build thereon a vigorous and happy state!" he exclaimed.[18]

Yoakum's real achievement and the key to his *History*'s resounding success lay in his masterful use of documentary sources. He began his research as early as 1850, some even speculate 1849. In a letter to Thomas J. Rusk in 1853, he wrote that he had been "two or three years engaged in collecting materials, and preparing a history of Texas." In January 1854, he wrote Houston: "I am constantly employed in my history. I find it much more troublesome and laborious than I expected, having often to consult a dozen works on a page. . . . I want to have everything correct."[19] Moreover, Yoakum recognized the relative quality of various sources. He used numerous personal accounts, but observed that they had their drawbacks: "The accounts [of the San Jacinto battle] vary considerable, from the fact that no one of the eye-witnesses, however impartial, could himself see the tenth part of what occurred during the 20th and 21st."[20]

This devotion to scrupulous research and annotated documentation benefited Yoakum's reputation in several ways. It set him apart among his contemporaries as being on the cutting edge, scientific and objective in his methods. It delighted fellow ideologues because his work offered them a meticulously documented and well-constructed justification of the ideology of westward expansion and empire, and its professional quality led later historians not to look too closely at his ideological biases. Consequently, his *History* incorporated the elements of his democratic ideology—the racism, the republicanism, and the expansionism—into the, presumably, objective record.

Perhaps in testimony to the thoroughness with which admiration of Yoakum's method obscured recognition of his biases, the modern reaction to his *History of Texas* was more sanguine than that of his contemporaries. Initial reaction demonstrated vividly the influence of politics on Texans' expectations as well as an increasing lack of consensus, generally, about what properly constituted good history writing. Immediately after the release of the first edition in 1855, the *Dallas Herald* criticized Yoakum's inability to escape his "biases and sympathies" for "his bosom friend" Sam Houston "so as to give an impartial and unprejudiced narrative." If his account of San Jacinto was a sample of his work, the public would have to "look to some future historian beyond the influence of living actors" to present "a faithful and unbiased account of them." The *Texas Almanac,* in 1856, conceded that "Yoakum's late valuable work gives us some satisfactory account of the first discovery and settlement of Texas." Later articles in 1859, 1860, and 1861 accused him of writing to Sam Houston's tune.[21] Contentions that the *Almanac's* publisher, Willard Richardson, or David G. Burnet authored the accusations seemed to be borne out when the attacks ceased after Houston's resignation as governor in 1861. Ashbel Smith lent credence to the idea that the *Almanac's* attacks were essentially political when, bitter over a series of articles in the *Galveston News* criticizing Anson Jones, he called Yoakum's *History* "concocted—Hasty prejudice, ignorant," and without regard to the available sources. Smith claimed that it was incorrect, incomplete, and false on the important events in history, "a burlesque of history, hardly accurate enough for the columns of a daily newspaper." Peter W. Gray, to whom the work was dedicated, was not overly generous in his praise either, saying it was "faithful and just as far as it goes" while conceding that it would be a standard in the future. He criticized Yoakum for error of expression and grammar and thought his style "too unpretentious" for his subject.

Outside Texas, reviews were more favorable; nevertheless, they reflected the American audience's continued preference for literary style. One of the earliest reviews, appearing in *DeBow's Review* in 1857, praised Yoakum for his collation of existing material as well as much new material. A review in *Harper's* the same year described the work as having been "prepared with painstaking diligence, and though without pretensions to grace or vivacity of style," it was "an important contribution to American History." A reviewer for *Putnam's* believed the books could have been written in "a more graphic and spirited" style and that the events of San Jacinto deserved "a somewhat less calm and summary enumeration" but agreed with other critics in praise of Yoakum's "diligence" and "perspicuous narrative." Yoakum's writing, wrote this critic, could not be called "classic" and displayed "no keen dissection of human motive" nor rose "to any stately and philosophic progression" but was "simple and clear, going direct and business-like to the point, and rarely confusing the facts it handles."[22]

Later historians were generally more effusive. Hubert Howe Bancroft thought Yoakum's history "one of the best, if not the best, history of Texas." Bancroft cited its completeness, dismissed the charges of Houston's influence, and considered minor errors unimportant to the work's value. In 1898, Seth Shepard and A. T. McKinney, two contributors to Wooten's *Compre-*

hensive History of Texas, excused defects in Yoakum's *History* as due to lack of necessary materials at the time and praised his "literary skill, painstaking accuracy, and the impartiality with which he reproduced the leading facts of [Texas'] growth and development." Wooten himself, while attempting to correct some of Yoakum's inaccuracies, reprinted his *History* in its entirety, stating that he could not improve upon it substantially enough to supersede it. The same year, C. W. Raines, like others, noted the deficiencies of Yoakum's coverage of the colonial era but concluded that with whatever defects it may have had, it was "the accepted standard of authority" for that time. Z. T. Fulmore, in 1935, wrote that Yoakum's *History* was "known and consulted by writers of history the world over, and regarded as the standard of the period which it covers." In 1945, Herbert Gambrell asserted that "[Yoakum] achieved a degree of objectivity unusual for the amateur historian, and literary style not often equaled by the professional," and Eugene C. Barker considered Yoakum's *History* the first "to meet the standards of professional historians."[23] Thus, at mid-twentieth century, the romantic narrative, albeit well documented, represented the hallmark in Texas history writing.

The writing of Yoakum, like that of Gouge and Navarro, exhibited the signs of a changing intellectual climate. Careful consideration of his work, and its reception, suggests that both the paradigm for writing history and the audience to whom it was directed were shifting. Although his style found favor with later historians, it seems to have been a bit dry for the taste of his contemporaries. In many ways, Yoakum was typical of romantic historians in America in the nineteenth century known as "patricians." He was a classically educated lawyer who undertook the writing of history in "days and nights stolen from other pursuits."[24] His philosophy of history and politics reflected the democratic ideals of Jefferson and Jackson. His themes reflected the basic assumptions that had guided the nation since the late eighteenth century, assumptions about patriotism, God, morality, and Anglo-American progress. He chose for his project a comprehensive history of his subject, one filled with bloody battles and heroic deeds. His style, though subdued, was unquestionably romantic. Much was made by contemporaries of his attention to sources and footnotes. Yoakum was not the first to use primary sources or footnotes; he was not, as some have claimed, the first to recognize that Texas had a history prior to the French intrusion in 1685; and he was as biased as his predecessors. He received acclaim and approbation denied them because his audience perceived him in different ways than it had earlier Texas historians. William Kennedy had written a carefully documented general history, but documentation was secondary to style in the mind of American audiences in 1841; they looked for a good story after the manner of Irving or Prescott.

Moreover, Kennedy had written for a British audience, not an American one. Henderson Yoakum, notably, wrote for a Texas audience, not a national one.

Much was made of Yoakum's scholarship because people paid attention to it. This was due, in part, to increased interest in research and documentation of historical works in the 1850s, making them seem more scientific. It may also have been due, in Yoakum's case, to the fact that, unlike his predecessors, he was a resident of Texas, not a visitor. He had moved there in 1845, a few years before he began writing his history, and was well established when he published it. His two volumes might be considered as promotional as earlier histories but in a different way. They were not written to promote personal interests, as were the histories of the 1830s, nor to promote political interests, as were the histories of the 1840s. Instead, he provided Texans with a documented and competently argued justification for their identity. Because it was born of ideology rather than expediency, for all its scholarship, his was the first genuinely romantic history of Texas. He attempted to bring the Texas Revolution within the canon of American Revolutionary myth, and he perpetuated the notion that right principles always triumph. The success of the Texas Revolution proved the virtue of the Texas republic compared to the "ignorance and despotism" of the Spanish and Mexicans. The success of energetic, noble-minded individuals, like Austin and Houston, proved that commitment to liberty and independence would bring prosperity to the Western wilderness. The growth of Texas proved that American principles of government were superior to others. Providence sanctioned this success because "enterprising, industrious, thrifty" American farmers had replaced the "savages" and, by developing the wilderness of Texas, were achieving the "great ends" of God. However romantic assumptions about God and right principles were, Yoakum made them seem irrefutable. His history was a turning point. It marked the beginning of the institutionalization of Texas' mythistory.[25]

5 ⋆ Lost Cause

Texas History, 1860–80

In the decade following the publication of Yoakum's *History,* two major events occurred that affected the writing of Texas history: the Civil War and the publication of Charles Darwin's *On the Origin of Species.* They influenced not only the way Texans thought about the past but also methods of writing about it. In a broader sense they influenced the relationship of Texas history to American history. In the United States, the Civil War stimulated interest in the whole field of American history, especially the study of the early national period and the foundations of the Union that the war presumably was fought to preserve. Though the struggle seemed "to banish for a season the study of the past," wrote the editor of the *Historical Magazine* in 1862, "our past history, now more than ever, claims, and is receiving, the attention of thinking men." Another contributor wrote soon after the war: "It is really only now that we are beginning to know for certain what were the undoubted facts in our revolutionary history of 1776."[1]

Certainly in Texas, the Civil War banished "for a season" the study of the past. No significant studies of state history appeared during the 1860s. Following the war a Southerner predicted that the history of the conflict would be written by Northerners.[2] In Texas the Civil War produced accounts of military campaigns and personal experiences but no critical studies of Texas' involvement in it. Published works between 1860 and 1875 included Rev. Nicholas A. Davis's *The Campaign from Texas to Maryland* (1863); Augustine Joseph Hickey Duganne's *Camps and Prisons: Twenty Months in the Department of the Gulf* (1865); Theophilus Noel's *A Campaign from Santa Fe to the Mississippi* (1865); William Williston Heartsill's *Fourteen Hundred and 91 Days in the Confederate Army* (1874–76); and Joseph Palmer Blessington's *The Campaigns of Walker's Texas Brigade* (1875).

When Texas histories did begin to appear again, they reflected the effects of both the outcome of the war and American society's newly elevated interest in science. A review of Texas histories written between 1855 and 1880 reveals that, indeed, its history was being written predominantly by Northerners, most of whom had taken up residence in the state prior to the war. Darwin's *On the Origin of Species* appeared in print in 1859, affecting the whole range of human knowledge. Charles Francis Adams declared that "a new epoch in the study of history" dated from its publication. Historians sought to successfully apply Darwin's methods to human history.[3] Americans, reflecting on their own national experience, were particularly attracted to Englishman Henry Buckle's thesis of the relationship between environment and the development of humanity, a theme becoming popular particularly with regional historians like Lyman Draper of Wisconsin, who embarked on a mission to rescue Western pioneers from oblivion by basing the reputations of his heroes firmly on fact so that their claim to fame could not be disputed.[4]

Still suffering the humiliation of being allied with a losing enterprise and the perception that they had been deprived of their self-determination by Reconstruction, Texans embraced the idea of rescuing their own heroes from oblivion and experienced a burst of renewed Texas nationalism, now flavored with the romantic nationalism that had spread through the South before the war. Following the Civil War, just as the upsurge of nationalism in American historiography naturally centered mainly on the romantic period of colonization and the struggle for American independence, so it was in Texas.[5] Among the first products of this renewed Texas nationalism and memorialization of national heroes were the works of DeWitt Clinton Baker and James Morphis.

James M. Morphis had come to Texas in 1846 from North Carolina and opened a law office in Paris, Texas, by the end of that year. He became active in politics and ran for United States Senate unsuccessfully against Louis T. Wigfall in 1859. When war came, Morphis served in the Confederate army at the rank of colonel. Afterward, he turned editor and traveling correspondent for the Galveston *Civilian* and the *Telegraph and Texas Register,* and by 1871 had settled down in Austin to write occasional sketches for the Austin *Daily Democratic Statesman.*[6]

When Morphis decided to gather his historical sketches into a book is unclear. In June 1874, the *Dallas Daily Herald,* announcing the forthcoming publication, reported that he had been for some time collecting facts and material for a complete history of Texas. The editors asserted that Morphis's twenty-five-year residence in Texas gave him "peculiar advantages" for the work of writing a history of the state. For his part, Morphis seemed motivated by a spirit of nationalism, both Texan and American, and a desire to dilute, if not completely dissolve, the inglorious memory of the Civil War by reviving the glorious memory of the Texas Revolution. His aim clearly was to give Texas, in the wake of the disheartening Lost Cause, a history of which Texans could be proud and which would remind the United States how fortunate it was to have Texas a part of it. "In a history of Texas," he wrote, "it is impossible to omit the four long weary years of war." But Morphis chose not to dwell on them or describe any battles, he explained to his readers, in the hope "that they may be remembered alone to prevent their recurrence." Further, he wrote, "the author's intention has been to show plainly and clearly to the world, that Texans were not only right in throwing off the government of Mexicans . . . but that they deserve the praise of all good people for changing a wilderness into green fields and happy homes." Morphis closed his preface with the assurance that his objective was "to amuse and interest, if not to instruct" and with a presumptuous quotation of verse, the gist of which was that his book was a memorial to the figures of history "that their names might not perish."[7]

Morphis's finished work was a scissors-and-paste rehash of Kennedy and Yoakum, combining narrative, whole texts of original documents, anecdotes, and creative dialogue. Literally putting words in the mouths of historical characters, such as an impassioned discussion between Sam Houston and his son over secession, made them more appealing to readers. Although the title proclaimed its comprehensiveness, Morphis devoted only two and a half pages to the entire period from 1685 to 1823. The vast bulk of the work was dedicated to the Texas Revolution. The Civil War received a dozen or so pages of conciliatory prose, which suggested that Texas had actually benefited from the outcome.[8] He followed his account of the war and Reconstruction with chapters on railroads, land titles, towns, rivers, agriculture, manufacturing, mining, and education, all in lively dialogue ending with an example of a Texas tall tale and a poetic benediction to Progress.

Morphis's history, not surprisingly, was well received by the reading public both at home and abroad. The New York *Turf, Field, and Farm* called it an "exceedingly clever production, in which the dignified and grave march of the muse of history is now and then pleasantly interrupted by those racy anecdotes so descriptive of frontier life." Following the book's release, the *Dallas Weekly Herald* praised it for its "humorous anecdotes," "droll" narration, and "pen pictures." The editors noted that apart from those features, the book also contained valuable information and historical data for those wishing to "read up" on Texas.[9]

Morphis's peculiar concoction of fact and fiction was not the only, or even the first, effort to fashion a usable past for post-Reconstruction Texas. Another antebellum immigrant, DeWitt Clinton Baker, turned out two historical works in the early 1870s. Their reception provided a large hint at the direction Texas history would take in the last quarter of the nineteenth century.

Baker, a native of Portland, Maine, and lifelong devotee of public education, settled in Austin in 1850. One of his earliest projects was the founding of the city's first public library. He variously engaged himself as a pharmacist, businessman, Bible society activist, essayist, poet, and tax collector, but his devotion to education was the thread that ran through all his activities and endeavors. Perhaps for this reason more than any other, he typified the changes occurring in the second half of the nineteenth century. Baker has been described as an urban progressive.[10] He was elected school trustee of Travis County in the 1850s or 1860s (depending on the account consulted) and appointed to the state school examining board by Governor E. J. Davis in 1872. During this period Baker became involved with the Republican administration's attempt to institute a public school system that mandated compulsory attendance, teacher certification, and uniform textbooks. In 1873, he published *A Brief History of Texas from Its Earliest Settlement* intended for use in schools. The state board adopted Baker's book, but revisions of the school law in 1873, over Davis's veto, began the dismantling of the public school system and effectively doomed the textbook. Texans complained that it expressed anti-Southern views, although no such bias is readily apparent.[11] The book's fate provided a revealing comment on what Texas readers wanted from their history. Elements of the cult of chivalry combined with the realities of frontier life to produce a distinctive version of Southern nationalism with which Texans identified themselves to some extent before and to an even greater extent after the Civil War.[12]

Having failed to appeal to the public with a traditional history but convinced of its importance, Baker tried another tactic calculated to be more palatable to his audience and, thus, more profitable to his publisher. His second book, *A Texas Scrapbook,* appeared in 1875. Like Morphis's *History,* it was a subscription book.[13] Although this venture proved a financial disaster to both author and publisher, Baker clearly intended to make money from its publication, and that aim no doubt influenced his approach to the endeavor. The book was a compilation designed for the casual reader. Like so many other volumes produced in the decade following the Civil War, it reflected the antiquarian's bent for "embalming the memory of the past" and "enshrining it in the present." The volume included anecdotes, poems, speeches, statistics, descriptions of climate and natural history, long lists of individuals, and biographical sketches of war dead, veterans of San Jacinto, and others who played some role in Texas history. With this format, Baker's compilation avoided any conclusions that might be construed as political bias and offered something for everyone: uninterpreted facts, colorful romantic narrative, and even sentimental poetry. Twentieth-century historians have praised it as a reference and research tool. However, Robert A. Calvert correctly identified its significance at its own time as representative of Texans' concept of history, which was characterized by anxiety to glorify their past and capture nostalgia for pioneer life that, with the proliferation of railroads and the appearance of the "machine in their Garden," many feared was disappearing.[14] In this respect, Baker's *Texas Scrapbook* very much represented the insecurity of changing times following the Civil War, when reality and new ideas were challenging long-held assumptions, and industrialization was threatening the long-cherished ideal of an agrarian republic.

As one result of the *Texas Scrapbook*'s lack of financial success, Barnes sold the plates for the book's engravings to another publisher, and all but four of the thirty-two engravings appeared in a later subscription history of Texas, Homer S. Thrall's *A Pictorial History of Texas, from the Earliest Visits of European Adventurers, to A.D. 1879 (1879)*. Thrall, a Methodist minister, educator, and Vermont native, was himself an example of a new breed of Texas historian in that, like Baker, he authored more than one publication on the subject, and like all his predecessors since Yoakum, he wrote as a resident of the state. He arrived in Texas from Ohio in late 1842 and began what would become a fifty-year ministry. As a circuit rider, he became acquainted with many settlers of Austin's original colony, veterans of the war for Texas independence, political leaders, and Texas Rangers, acquaintances to whom he attributed his interest in Texas history. At various times over the years he taught school and served as college trustee. Between 1872 and 1889, he published five widely read books related to Texas, the first being *A Brief History of Methodism in Texas* in 1872. As a teacher, Thrall evidently perceived, as had Baker, the need for a standard textbook on Texas history. His slender volume, *A History of Texas,* first appeared in 1876 and was later expanded and reprinted.[15]

In the preface to the 1876 volume, Thrall stated that his purpose was to give "a clear, concise, and accurate history of Texas." He admitted that such an aim precluded elaborate discussion or minuteness of detail.[16] The book could not have been mistaken for anything other than a textbook. He presented the text in numbered paragraphs that corresponded to questions at the bottom of the pages over the material contained in each paragraph. He offered little original research, relying primarily on the previous works of

Yoakum, Kennedy, Foote, and Holley and personal interviews. He opened
with the landing of La Salle, obviously believing, despite Yoakum's admoni-
tion that Texas history preceded that event, anything prior to be irrelevant to
the young minds of late–nineteenth-century Texas.

Probably as a reflection of the aftermath of the Civil War, Thrall treated
controversial subjects, such as slavery and Indians in the early Anglo-
American settlements, with studied neutrality. He avoided the suggestion
that most colonists actually approved of the slave trade or that the Mexican
government was oppressive in its enforcement of its prohibition.[17] Thrall devoted a total of two paragraphs to the matter and only about three pages to
the native tribes and Indian relations. In contrast, he devoted six pages to the
siege of the Alamo, in which he rejected Filisola's report that Travis had early
proposed surrender in exchange for the lives of his men. He gave three pages
to an account of the battle of San Jacinto.

In keeping with the highly condensed format, Thrall's style was terse. His
second history of Texas, *A Pictorial History of Texas,* was considerably more
colorful and attracted much more attention. It was largely promotional in the
same vein as immigrant guides of the late 1840s and 1850s: "To the hardy
poorman who expects to make his living by honest industry and to raise his
family where they will enjoy the advantages of good schools and churches,
probably no portion of the American continent offers such advantages as
Texas. Here labor is always in demand at a remunerative price; provisions are
cheap; here is land for those who wish either to lease or purchase; tenement
houses are furnished to farm laborers; and a permanent home may be acquired upon accommodating terms."[18] Although Thrall's *Pictorial History of
Texas* has been subsequently quoted by other writers, some contemporary
Texans took immediate and intense umbrage to it. In a review that appeared
in the *Galveston News,* Temple Houston issued a blistering indictment of the
work. "Its title to 'history' is fatally defective, because of its glaring inaccuracies and numerous errors," he ranted. Most of the errors he specifically cited
had to do with geographical descriptions and not history. Nevertheless,
Houston continued, "Its malicious insinuations stamp its author as a man
unfit to follow the exalted calling of the historian." Houston's numerous
charges included plagiarism and omission or slighting of individuals (mostly
lawyers or judges) whom he considered more worthy than those Thrall included in his "Biographical Sketches of Distinguished Characters in Texas."
In his passionate criticism, Houston revealed much about the degree to which
nativism colored the historic perception of many Texans: "It matters not in
my eyes what faults these brave men may have had, or how bitterly they hated
my father, they loved Texas, and that single fact throws a halo of brightness

around their memories, and I will not silently see their glorious names, resplendent with deeds done for Texas, sullied and clouded by the hand of an alien and a stranger. . . . I denounce his work as a stigma on the name of history, as a fraud on the people of Texas, as an insult to their intelligence, and as containing libelous attacks on the character of one of her dead soldiers."[19] Even though Thrall's work was not a great literary achievement nor a particularly scholarly or insightful history, its flaws did not warrant such vituperation. Such a reaction was again instructive of Texans' expectations of history and their sensitivity to any perceived criticism, which, if not more widespread, appeared at least more vocal than it had been earlier in the century.

One veteran of the Texas Revolution kinder in his criticism of Thrall was Reuben M. Potter, another self-styled historian. "Mr. Thrall deserves great credit for his efforts to keep alive the names of so many of the pioneers and veterans," he told M. A. Bryan in 1883.[20] As a historian, Potter represented one of the most obvious changes in the writing of Texas history to take place in the late nineteenth century. A New Jersey native, he came to his interest in Texas by way of Mexico, where, from 1827 to 1833, he worked as agent of a commercial house in Matamoros. During the Texas Revolution he successfully obtained a decree of amnesty from the Mexican government for twenty-one Texans held prisoner there. By 1837, he had become a Texas resident and served as a customs officer until 1845. He acted as a translator for the Texas government on various occasions and, as a member of the U.S. Quartermaster Department in San Antonio in 1861, was briefly imprisoned by Confederate forces under Ben McCulloch.

Following the Civil War, Potter did quite a bit of writing, which earned him a reputation as an authority on the Alamo. His short articles on the Texas Revolution began to appear in print as early as 1860.[21] Many of them appeared in Eastern papers and periodicals such as the *New York Times* and the *Magazine of American History* beginning in the late 1870s. Like Navarro, Potter confined his historical writing to a series of articles on specific topics rather than attempting a comprehensive history or a single volume. Like Navarro, he wrote chiefly to correct the record, and, also like Navarro, he wrote with the authority of an eyewitness but with the incisiveness of a clinician. "The details of the final assault [on the Alamo] have never been fully and correctly narrated, and wild exaggerations have taken their place in popular legend," he wrote in his earliest article to appear in *Magazine of American History.* "The reason will be obvious when it is remembered that not a single combatant of the last struggle from within the fort survived to tell the tale, while the official reports of the enemy were neither circumstantial nor reliable. When horror is intensified by mystery, the sure product is romance." Potter acknowledged that a great deal of collection, evaluation, and comparison of sources was necessary to arrive at a reliable conclusion about what actually happened. He pointed out flaws in Yoakum's highly respected account and asserted that statistical and direct data were necessary to obtain a clear historical understanding of events. "The account of the assault which Yoakum and others have adopted as authentic is evidently one which popular tradition has based on conjecture," he warned. To correct this situation, Potter offered detailed measurements and even a drawing of the layout of the Alamo that supported his own conclusions about what must have taken place. He tackled with aplomb one of the most sensitive and historically controversial issues concerning defenders of the Alamo. Although admitting that no small part of the group were ruffians and filibuster types, he noted that there were also "those fighting for the safety of their nearby families, and like Bonham and Crockett who had an honest faith in their espoused cause, and these, plus the situation, raised the lowest of the garrison to the thrill of patriots and made them braver and more courageous than they really were," an observation unnoted by Yoakum but remarkably similar to that of William Kennedy nearly forty years earlier.[22]

Also like Navarro, Potter was one of very few writers in the nineteenth century to recognize the contributions of Mexicans in the Texas Revolution and to deal with racial myths perpetuated by Anglo-American and European historians.[23] Essentially debunking the romantic explanation for the success of the Texan rebels, based on ideas of Providence and racial superiority, Potter, echoing Filisola, suggested that racism had less to do with the historical perception of Mexico than the dreadful mistakes of her individual leaders. "It was the *bad* luck of fools which rendered Mexico powerless and made Texas her match in spite of odds," he wrote in a historical essay in 1883. "They won for Mexico the loathing and contempt, and for Texas sympathy, of the civilized world, and in many direct and countless indirect ways tended to uphold the latter." Like Yoakum, Potter wrote more favorably of Sam Houston than most historians had up to that time. "The history of the Republic of Texas is much of it a history of popular illusion and Houston did more than any other one man to avert its ruinous effects," he wrote.[24] Although Potter's apparent and consistent high regard for Houston might easily be regarded as bias, his defense of the general did much to balance the treatment of Houston's role in Texas history to that date.

Another of Potter's important contributions to Texas history was his rationale for its study. From his earliest published articles on the subject, Potter perceived events in Texas in terms of their impact on the larger context of the United States and the world. "As Valmy was the parent of Jemmapes, and consequently the progenitor of Austerlitz and Waterloo, so San Jacinto begot Palo Alto, and Palo Alto begot Bull Run and Gettysburg. A small rock at the source may give a wide divergence to a river, and a petty contingency at a critical point may thus turn the course of history."[25] Potter's statement placed him among the first to offer a practical reason for studying Texas history beyond reiterating the themes of liberty, patriotism, progress, and manifest destiny. It also made him one of the first to treat Texas history as American history and to recognize its role in shaping that history. His insight seems to have had little effect. Ironically, Potter is probably better known for his sentimental poem "Hymn of the Alamo," written in 1836, than for his later articles on the Texas Revolution and republic. Although no figures are available for comparison, it is likely that Potter was not as widely read or nearly as well known as Mary Austin Holley among general readers. Yet, his articles were notably free of sentimental rhetoric. His direct approach to historical evidence and matter-of-fact style reflected a changing paradigm in history writing and readers as America neared the final decades of the nineteenth century.

The third quarter of the nineteenth century marked the beginning of changes in the American climate of opinion. Whereas the work of men like Darwin and Buckle redefined society's understanding of science and its application to human life, the American Civil War had a more immediate effect on history writing, particularly in the South—beforehand by inspiring historical defenses of the Cause, afterward by quieting Southern interest in history. As a contemporary of that era remarked on reading Charles Ramsdell's 1910 work on Reconstruction, "I have been rereading your *Reconstruction in Texas* and realize more than ever the great importance as a historical record. The present generation knows absolutely nothing of that period in our history, because it was so extremely painful to those who passed through it, that their pens refused to write of it, their tongues were silent from excessive emotion at the mere thought of trying to relate its humiliating experiences."[26] During more than a decade, from the beginning of the Civil War until near the end of Reconstruction, personal reminiscences, adventure stories, and biographies filled the void. Both new scientific theories and war challenged basic assumptions that had provided the themes and determined the subjects, methods, and style of history writing throughout the nineteenth century. People of the Confederacy had to come to terms with the reality of the Lost Cause despite their long-held conviction that right always triumphed. Texas reacted with a renewed sense of romantic nationalism, nativism, and interest in its origins.

Texas historians during this period were Texas residents more often than not, but significantly most had emigrated from Northern states. Many concentrated their efforts on particular aspects of Texas history rather than on comprehensive works. Men like Gouge, Yoakum, and Potter went to some lengths to be scholarly in their methods and scrupulously thorough in their collection, evaluation, and documentation of sources. At least two authors treated the role of Tejanos in Texas history. At the same time, the era of the revolution and republic was more romanticized than ever before, for emotional and ideological purposes instead of pragmatic ones. Texans found the past useful in supplying themselves with a positive sense of identity following the humiliation of the Civil War and Reconstruction. They reacted unfavorably, at times even vehemently, against the history written by men they might have considered scalawags. They turned for validation of their identity to the last comprehensive history written before the war, a history written by a Jacksonian ideologue, one that did not challenge or threaten Southern antebellum ideals. This was the history that became the standard for school texts in the 1870s and was still proclaimed the definitive history of Texas at the turn of the century. The Texas myth had come of age. It had become entwined with Texas history, no longer because it was expedient but because it defined how Texans saw themselves, as the embodiment of their collective memory.

6 ★ Every Texan an Historian

Discernible changes took place in Texas history writing during the last two decades of the nineteenth century. Whether they constituted progress depends on one's definition of the term. Civil War and Reconstruction contributed to these changes in two important ways. The aftermath of the Civil War produced a nostalgia for the triumphant revolutionary era and a kinship with the states of the former Confederacy that had not previously existed even during the war itself.[1] But other events in the intellectual history of the United States, generally, also contributed to developments in Texas historiography after 1880, among them the growth of the profession of history and the profound effect of Frederick Jackson Turner's frontier thesis.[2]

By the early 1880s, the shift in dominance from the amateur to professional historian had occurred, yet the traditional American view that history was entertainment or moral instruction remained a powerful influence. A new generation of historians trained in scientific methods scoffed at George Bancroft's romanticism and religiosity. They applied the latest scientific methods, but they still tried to assimilate American history to a pattern of unchanging principles. The main difference, at least one historian has suggested, had more to do with method than conviction. The idea of moral progress persisted, but the mode changed from literary artistry to scientific procedures.[3] Earlier historians had transcendental faith in progress; the newer generation had facts to support the hypothesis. The assumption remained the same. Scientific history, nevertheless, involved more than a critical approach to evidence; it subordinated romantic values to a scientific spirit that was impersonal, collaborative, secular, "impatient of mystery," and concerned with the relation of things to one another rather than their relation to some ultimate reality. These new realistic historians did not necessarily exceed the romantic historians in factual accuracy. They sought to correct the subjective errors of romantic history by letting facts speak for themselves. They welcomed specialization and monographs on limited subjects. In order to handle

subjects beyond the research of a single specialist, they published large collaborative works. They detached themselves from their subjects and did not
immerse themselves in the mood and emotions of historical situations. To
avoid the pitfall of subjectivity, they refrained, with varying degrees of success, from passing moral judgment on their subjects.[4] They were university
trained, and perfect objectivity was the "noble dream" they set as their goal.

Evidence of both the paradigm shift and resistance to change manifested
itself in Texas historical writing in the last two decades of the nineteenth century. While professional history found its way into the university, the impulse
toward romantic nationalism devolved into nostalgia during the Gilded Age.
Americans, including Texans, turned to nostalgia not just because it provided
escapism, but also because, as one intellectual historian has explained, nostalgia, in its creative manifestations, helped people legitimize new political
orders, rationalize adjustments and perpetuation of old social hierarchies,
and construct acceptable new systems of thought and values. These creative
manifestations took the form of all kinds of public monuments in Texas and
throughout the United States, the refurbishment and perpetuation of myths,
and sometimes, the development of conflicting or contradictory traditions in
the same locale.[5] Just as Americans looked back nostalgically to the Revolutionary War, Texans turned to their own revolution and produced an im-
pressive list of heroes now worthy of memorializing, even some of previously
dubious reputation, such as Sam Houston. Such heroes, burnished in the sentimental glow of the past, belonged more aptly to the romantic history of the
patricians than to the new historians of the scientific age.

Patrician history, exemplified by the romantic historians Motley, Bancroft,
Prescott, and Parkman, retained the discursive, narrative form, whereas professionals eschewed all literary pretensions. The stylistic ornaments, vivid
scenes, and epic subjects of romantic history, however, were simply more cap-
tivating to general audiences than were the unembellished scientific facts.
As romanticism gradually gave way to realism, professional historians would
find an audience, but it would not be the contemporary reading public, who
had overwhelmingly preferred fiction for generations. Statistics tell the story.
A phenomenal increase in reading occurred in the United States between 1830
and 1850, as indicated in the estimates of book production in dollars prepared
by historians of American publishing, and historical novels ranked high
among the popular best-sellers of their day. The single Texas book to make
the list (meaning it sold more than 175,000 copies) was Kendall's *Narrative of
the Texan Santa Fe Expedition,* in 1844. The most important titles in the fields
of history and historical fiction were all published before the end of the Civil
War, and "they all retained their hold on the public for many decades to

come." In fact, the number of new titles and new editions of history books dropped from 114 in 1869 to 72 in 1880, whereas general literature and essays increased by almost identical numbers during the same time period.[6] In the waning years of the nineteenth century, the critical historians appealed to a different audience than did the patrician historians they were displacing. Professionals replaced the patricians as the history-writing elite, but they did not write for a democratic audience. The new elite found an equally elite audience—themselves.

The very gradual shift from romanticism to realism in historical method was tentative but present in Texas during the last quarter of the nineteenth century, particularly with the establishment of the Department of History at the University of Texas. Resistance to change also continued to be evident, particularly in the emergence of a prodigiously creative nostalgia. Perhaps the first evidence of the new scientific method applied to Texas history was the work of Californian Hubert Howe Bancroft. Bancroft represented changes in multiple ways. He was detached from his subject both literally and figuratively. He neither resided in nor visited for any length of time in Texas, and he endeavored to produce a history that would present readers with all the facts from which they could make their own deductions and form their own opinions. "It was ever my aim to tell the story clearly and concisely, taking a common-sense practical view of things, and arranging them in natural sequence," he explained in a defense of his work.[7] Bancroft also represented the new methods of critical history by assembling a staff of specialists to assist him with the research and writing of a mammoth comprehensive history. In fact, he considered this "system" to be his greatest achievement and contribution. "My system," he wrote, "applies only to the accumulation and arrangement of evidence upon the topics of which I write, and consists in the application of business methods and the division of labor to those ends. By its aid I have attempted to accomplish in one year what would require ten years by ordinary methods; or on a complicated and extensive subject to collect practically all the evidence, when by ordinary methods a lifetime of toil would yield only a part. . . . In long and complicated subjects to which my method is applicable, and which cannot be successfully treated by any other, I am inclined to regard the division of labor as an advantage in itself."[8]

His "system" combined the proclivities of the antiquarian with the methods of the professional historians. In his effort to "exhaust" the subject, Bancroft produced, as he intended, a summation and critical digest of all published knowledge concerning the natural, cultural, and political history of the entire western half of the North American continent. He began the work in 1874 after retiring from a highly successful career as a bookseller, printer, and publisher, and by 1890 he had published thirty-nine large volumes. He had started collecting Californiana about 1859 for a *Pacific Coast Handbook* he published with the idea that the editor would find it convenient to have all the books on the subject brought together. His collection grew by leaps and bounds, partly because he realized that limiting research to the confines of a state or national border was impossible if it were to be historically and geographically sound, and partly because he concentrated on content rather than format, collecting every item with the slightest bearing on the subject. In 1869, in order to house his mammoth project, he erected a building that became known as the "history-factory." He hired a staff of six hundred to assist with the collecting, research, and writing. Bancroft himself edited.[9]

Bancroft's two volumes, *History of the North Mexican States and Texas, 1531-1889,* appeared in 1883 and 1889 respectively.[10] They were enormously important to Texas history for several reasons but never much appreciated by contemporary Texans. Not only had Bancroft amassed far more sources than any of his predecessors, but he was the first historian of the nineteenth century to treat Texas history in a larger historical and geographical context, that of Mexican history as well as the history of the American West.[11] He also accomplished what Yoakum had first attempted by beginning Texas history with the explorations of Hernan Cortés. His research included Mexican sources to which Yoakum had alluded. Like the trained historians of the scientific school, he focused on institutions in an attempt to convey a sense of Texas' growth beyond its rough frontier and revolutionary epoch toward a more cosmopolitan future. He abandoned almost entirely the portrayal of history as adventure. He did, nevertheless, portray Texas as an example of Anglo-American progress. He still viewed history as the anticipation of empire, indicative perhaps of the Gilded Age; only his villains had changed. Instead of savage Indians and tyrannical Mexicans, civilization had to conquer speculators, railroads, monopolies, plutocrats, and other assorted evils of the commercial republic.

The first volume covered the Spanish Southwest in general with emphasis on Texas. The second volume covered the history of Texas in the nineteenth century through 1888, with additional chapters on education, industry, commerce, and railroads. Eleven chapters dealt with the Mexican border states. Though there were errors, the two volumes comprised, without question, the most comprehensive and critical treatment of Texas ever to be written. In the terms under which Bancroft originally approached his task, it remains the best critical digest of published knowledge available through 1888.

Bancroft considered his project no less ambitious than the works of Edward Gibbon, Francis Parkman, or George Bancroft and just as worthy of fame. He realized that his endeavor would not likely be profitable considering the immense cost of its production. He expected, however, to be recognized as a scholar and literary figure and respected among the elite of the world's most learned. This desire was evident in many of his essays, such as the chapter entitled "History Writing" in his *Essays and Miscellany,* published in 1890.[12] These works clearly revealed that he not only collected books, but he also read them. The quality of his personal essays, not to mention the sheer magnitude of his work, made such expectations seem reasonable and well deserved. Bancroft went to great lengths to market his history and to ensure a favorable critical reception, and, eventually, the venture did yield a sizable profit.

But Bancroft never received the respect and recognition for which he yearned. In Texas as elsewhere, critics focused on the ethics of his "system," which, in their view, credited him with the work of others. In 1895, C. W. Raines stated, "Were I restricted to a single book on Texas, I would, without hesitation, take Bancroft's *History . . .*" The *Quarterly of the Texas State Historical Association,* however, commenting on an article by William Alfred Morris concerning Bancroft's twenty-volume *History of the Pacific States,* made much of Morris's allegation that the *North Mexican States and Texas* were not Bancroft's work at all and belittled his role, if accurate, as managing editor: "Mr. Bancroft's lack of frankness, his failure to apprehend the ethics of authorship, could not fail to bring discredit upon his work." The writer of this note went on to concede that though Bancroft's history of Texas contained errors, and though even he omitted extant material unknown to him, the historian of the future would have to work upon the foundation he had laid. Ever after, the history of Texas would have to be thought of in its relation to the history of Spanish North America.[13]

Bancroft's critical reception underscored the growing elitism of professional historians. They tended to dismiss his work as local history and *Western* local history at that. Bancroft's fate haunts Texas historians even today. Texas history has never lived down this charge, possibly because Texans themselves continue to promote the image of Texas as a place apart. Critics who denounced Bancroft for his "history-factory," ignored the similarity between his methods and those of young men from European "seminaries," who were establishing "literary factories" at Eastern universities like Harvard, or Leopold Von Ranke, who used the work of countless graduate students in the writing of his universal history, or any number of other scholarly cooperative projects of the same period.[14]

In fact, Texas history in the last decade of the nineteenth century was the subject of a number of cooperative "memorial" or "vanity" histories, all of them by amateurs. The most voluminous of these was another massive comprehensive history compiled by Dudley G. Wooten, a lawyer who had been educated at Johns Hopkins, was instrumental in chartering the University of Texas, and was a founder of the Texas State Historical Association. Wooten's endeavor represented Texas' historical consciousness in the late nineteenth century in its combining of adherence to romantic principles with the more recent scientific method in the gathering of specialized monographs, in its post-Reconstruction nostalgia, and—possibly as an extension of that nostalgia—in its bigness. The work consisted of two oversized volumes totaling nearly 1,800 pages. As evidence of Wooten's romantic orientation, the compilation began with a reprint of Yoakum's *History of Texas,* which Wooten and others attempted to correct through the addition of annotations, but which he insisted could not be substantially improved upon. The remainder of the voluminous text consisted of chronologically arranged essays and memoirs on Texas history from Austin's colony to 1897, some of them book-length. Wooten concluded with a lengthy summary of the significance of the last fifty years of the century and pages of statistical tables. His own contributions on Spanish and Mexican land titles, Texas land laws, and the results of Texas' progress since statehood were praised as "scholarly, statistical, and devoid of moral judgement," which a reviewer in *The Dial* deemed "noteworthy contributions to the history of the Southwest." C. W. Raines, reviewing the work for the *Quarterly of the Texas State Historical Association* called it the "New Yoakum." Probably without realizing the irony in his observation, Raines wrote, "Considering its conglomerate character, this work is something more than a history in the ordinary acceptance of the term."[15]

Raines, state librarian of Texas and generally considered a professional historian, reiterated earlier critics of Yoakum, stating that "with whatever defects it might have, [it] is the accepted standard of authority today, having more merit than any other history of the state ever written by a Texan."[16] With respect to the objectivity question so much in vogue in the late nineteenth century, Raines noted that Wooten had been "an ardent secessionist and an honest doctrinaire of the Calhoun school of State Rights politics" but had nevertheless produced "the most impartial history of Texas for the period covered that has ever been written." The most revealing comment by Raines, however, might be his review of Oran Roberts's contribution on the Civil War and Reconstruction: "Reconstruction was the hideous nightmare worse than war for Texans. The exasperating events of this period are given without loss of temper, but the tyranny of the Davis administration does not escape recital and the proper condemnation." A myth for coping with the Civil War and

Reconstruction had obviously been immediately constructed and embraced by amateur and professional historians alike. "Calmness" of recital they equated with detachment and objectivity. Raines criticized Roberts only for his unscientific probing for the "philosophy of events." He concluded by comparing Wooten's *Comprehensive History* with Justin Winsor's *Narrative and Critical History of North America.*[17]

Wooten's collaboration with publisher William Scarff was, in essence, a memorial to the events of Texas history and those who participated in them. It was by far the most comprehensive of such memorials, but it was certainly not the only one. Andrew Jackson Sowell and John W. Wilbarger, veterans of the Indian wars, produced books that were part compilation and part chronicle. The contributions to these works consisted not of specialized research but of memoirs and recollections.[18] These books characterized numerous works, large and small, published between 1883 and 1899.

Personal journals and reminiscences found their way into print during this period in record numbers. As the revolutionary generation aged and began to die out, Texans became conscious of the need to preserve the memory of men and deeds. In an effort to gain support for the preservation of Texas history, all kinds of personal accounts were regarded as history and used to keep alive these memories. This outpouring of nostalgia in the guise of history became more democratic than ever. Authors came from every walk of life. Women, too, recorded and published their memoirs. Some of these authors retained the exciting, colorful style of romanticism, but some, like Will James, studiously avoided the sensational and tried to give straightforward accounts.[19]

One of these personal memoirs, which the author expanded into an attempt at comprehensive history, was that of John Henry Brown. John H. Jenkins called Brown's *History of Texas from 1685 to 1892* "the earliest comprehensive history of Texas written by an active participant." Brown had served as an Indian fighter with the Texas Rangers, as a colonel in the Texas militia during the Mexican War, as adjutant general under McCulloch during the Civil War, as mayor of Dallas, and as a leader in drafting the 1876 Texas Constitution. At various times he had been a printer and newspaper publisher. He spent fifty years collecting material for his history and four years writing it. Brown acknowledged the current demand for history based on facts and information: "Eschewing fiction and exaggeration and guided by the spirit of truth and justice, this work is given to the people of Texas." However, Brown provided an example of the historical consciousness that subscribed to unchanging principles of earlier days with the opening sentences of his introduction, in which he dismissed the significance of any events in Texas prior to Anglo-American settlement in 1822: "From the latter year we trace all of

Texas identified with those principles of liberty, and representative, constitutional government held, at least by all English-speaking people, to be essential to the continued progress and happiness of mankind." One reviewer wrote that it was "the most thorough, impartial and accurate history of Texas ever published." Another stated that his work could "be scrutinized in vain to find a deliberate utterance antagonistic to public or private virtue or unfaithful to the glory of Texas," which, as some have pointed out, was the work's chief shortcoming.[20] Despite his claims of impartiality, Brown was utterly biased and selective in his presentation of facts and devoted to romantic assumptions about liberty, progress, and Providence.

The efforts to publish standard history textbooks in the third quarter of the nineteenth century continued in the final decades. The passage of the Public School Act, as well as the widespread call for history instruction in schools and universities, inspired half a dozen or so textbooks in the 1890s. These histories seemed to be written more with a purpose than a thesis, and they were authored exclusively by amateur historians. They were characterized by a patriotic emphasis and provincial orientation. Their purpose, according to Anna J. Pennybacker in *A New History of Texas for Schools,* was to present "varied and romantic scenes" that would "cultivate true patriotism." Anna Pennybacker was a public school teacher from Palestine, Texas, whose textbook enjoyed great popularity. First published in 1888, it was revised and reprinted in 1895, 1898, and 1900. The publishing team of William Scarff and Dudley Wooten, having completed their opus, published an ambitious school history in 1899. In it Wooten acknowledged a debt to H. H. Bancroft and Justin Winsor, as well as a score of "specialists" on various aspects of Texas history, including William Corner, Adele Looscan, Andrew J. Houston, and E. T. Dumble.[21] Mary M. Brown's *A Condensed History of Texas for Schools* (1895), which relied heavily on her husband John Henry's *History of Texas,* was intended to assist the teacher "to kindle the fire of patriotism in the breast of the pupils." Brown himself published *A School History of Texas from Its Discovery in 1685 to 1893* (1893) in the same year that the second volume of his *History* came out. Even more nostalgic was *Under Six Flags, the Story of Texas* (1897) by M[ollie] E[velyn] M[oore] Davis, a writer of fiction and poetry. "The history of Texas is far more than a romantic legend," she wrote. "It is a record of bold conceptions and bolder deeds; the story of the discoverer penetrating unknown wildernesses; of the pioneer matching his strength against the savage; of the colonist struggling for his freedom and his rights."[22] Davis's little volume illustrated the acceptance of nostalgia in place of history in late-nineteenth-century Texas. Even more important, Davis directly addressed the frontier influence in shaping Texans' and Americans' concept of the meaning of history.

Frederick Jackson Turner's frontier thesis, first expressed in an address to the American Historical Association in 1891, was America's most popular explanation of itself, and, according to historians Michael Kraus and David D. Joyce, it has held that place from its publication in 1893 to the present. With Turner, Texas history became not just America's history but the image the world at large carried of American history, because Texas epitomized the American character as Americans believed it to be: rugged, individualistic, optimistic, and democratic. These were the unchanging principles to which American historians, whether romantic or scientific, whether amateur or professional, paid homage.[23]

Professional historians in Texas shared this concept of American and Texas history as surely as the average citizen. As historian John Higham has observed, the argument sparked by the Turner thesis over the influence most responsible for shaping American history and forming a distinctive national character never spread beyond the confines of American universities. In the popular mind, the vision of the pioneer as the quintessential American never wavered.[24] Nevertheless, the establishment of the Department of History at the University of Texas did have an impact in the last years of the nineteenth century. The movement in Texas toward a uniform historical method received possibly its greatest impetus from two professors who, with Wooten and others, helped establish the Texas State Historical Association. They were George Pierce Garrison and Lester Bugbee.

Garrison, who as the chair of the newly created Department of History at the University of Texas in 1889 initiated the professionalization of Texas historiography, was among the first professional Texas historians to incorporate Turner's thesis into his interpretation of the state's history. He was professionally trained as a historian at the University of Chicago and had moved to Texas from Georgia in 1874. He carried with him the influence of his Southern heritage, and his writing reflected the influence of traditional nineteenth-century themes of moralism and patriotism. He also exhibited the influence of late-nineteenth-century American expansionism and naturalistic trends such as the theory of Social Darwinism, which became associated with the concept of "a new manifest destiny." Yet, unlike previous Texas historians, who saw nationalism almost exclusively in local terms, Garrison, significantly, portrayed Texas history as an aspect of United States history. "The best history is that which gives the clearest explanation of the unfolding of national life," he wrote.[25] Thus, he succeeded where Bancroft failed to inspire Texas historians to interpret and write about Texas not only as part of a larger event—the westward movement of the United States—but also as part of the by-then prevalent idea of a larger manifest destiny.

In his most important local study, *Texas: A Contest of Civilizations,* Garrison revealed the influences of nationalism, social evolution, manifest destiny, and the germ theory, which had been advocated much earlier in the nineteenth century by Henry Adams, John Burgess, and other scholars who had studied in Germany. Garrison was not the first to introduce the notion of racial superiority in Texas historiography, but he lent it the authority of the "scientific" historian. His writing represented well the contradiction between scientific history and America's tenacious devotion to unchanging principles of moralism, nationalism, and destiny. "In Garrison," recalled H. Y. Benedict, former president of the University of Texas, "the scientific historian was ever subordinate to the patriotic citizen. He . . . firmly believed that history revealed an unceasing moral purpose running through the ages . . . and that the experience of the past could profitably be brought to bear on the problems of the future." He believed that the advance into the West produced the distinctive characteristics of Americanism, and he saw Texas history as part of this westward movement. He also believed that natural selection had produced in the pioneers their energy, adventurousness, and willingness to take risks and endure hardships, and he believed that these rugged individualists were nearly exclusively Anglo-American and had brought the germ of institutions inherited from England into the West well before the flow of European immigration. He analyzed the problem of nationalism and sectionalism in this light and concluded that the nationalizing tendencies evidenced by United States westward expansion were too strong to be overcome.[26]

Despite his rather romantic view of nationalism, Garrison's potential influence as a scientific historian was mitigated even more by pressure from conservative Texas political sentiment. Prodded by citizens embittered by the Civil War and Reconstruction, the Texas legislature adopted a resolution on June 9, 1897, demanding an investigation into teaching at the University of Texas that allegedly failed to emphasize support for Southern traditions and institutions.[27] The effect on the future of Texas history writing was devastating. Faced with the imminent destruction of the history department at the university, Garrison capitulated. Texans conceived of themselves as part of the solid South, and they wanted a Southern history. He succeeded in institutionalizing professional history and making Texas history the subject of scholarly study, but Garrison did not entirely depart from the romantic legacy that Anglo-Americans conquering the frontier imparted to Texas prior to the Civil War, the pressure of Southern nationalism, or the influence of his own Southern upbringing. The programs he established bore the stamp of these factors as well as his professional philosophy.

One of Garrison's students, Lester Gladstone Bugbee, contributed significantly to the professionalization of Texas history and, along with Garrison, helped lay the groundwork for a "Texas School of History." Although Garrison viewed Texas as part of the American West, he also acknowledged it as part of a distinct Southwest region, a primarily geographical concept important for its recognition of the Spanish heritage of that portion of the United States. Bugbee represented the bridge between the nationalistic emphasis of Garrison and the regional approaches to Texas history beginning with the Southwestern emphasis.[28]

Lester Bugbee was born in Texas, the first historian of the nineteenth century to claim the distinction. He attended the University of Texas, where he completed a master's thesis on the history of Stephen F. Austin's colony, using the records of the General Land Office and documents published in the histories of Foote and Yoakum. At Columbia University he came under the influence of scholars Herbert Levi Osgood, John Bassett Moore, E. R. A. Seligman, John W. Burgess, and William A. Dunning. In his brief career as a professional historian, Bugbee produced a relatively small amount of published material, articles that appeared between 1897 and 1900 in scholarly journals, but the influence of his work proved significant. Bugbee helped change the romantic tone of historical writing about the period of Texas' colonization, revolution, and republic and the causes of the Mexican War.

But, appropriately, Bugbee's greatest service was perhaps as an educator, not just of university students but of ordinary Texans whom he advised and encouraged. Editors of women's magazines sought his opinion, and amateur historians sought his endorsements. Echoing William Prescott, they obviously believed "interest" to be of paramount importance in writing history. "What do you consider the best text on Texas history?" inquired one member of a women's club. "Mrs. Pennybacker is not authentic, but exceedingly interesting. . . . What are the most interesting things written about Texas?" Anna Pennybacker herself assured him that she would be delighted if he could deem hers the best textbook extant on Texas history for the common schools. She needed recommendations, she said, "from the leading Texas school" concerning her book to convince the school board to buy it.[29]

Garrison and Bugbee probably made a greater impact on Texas history in organizing the Texas State Historical Association than in their writing. Garrison realized that given the political pressures on the university, history could be promoted in Texas only by getting as many citizens involved as possible. "Our intention," he told former governor Oran Roberts, "is to send circular invitations to a number of persons from whom we may hope for efficient cooperation throughout the state to be present, or, at any rate, to become members, and we wish to have the names of a few well-known citizens of Texas signed to the call." He was also smart enough to realize that the best way to disarm potential enemies was to invite them into one's own camp. Hence, when he resolved to form a historical society, he appealed to history-minded citizens and high-ranking politicians. The pages of the *Quarterly* were filled with reminiscences and nostalgia of countless amateur historians whom Garrison, as editor, instructed in scientific methods as he published their work. Roberts became the Association's first president.[30]

Given Garrison's background and worldview, it would be difficult to say whether he succumbed to conservative political pressure or won it over to his view when, in fact, there was not a vast gulf between them. But Garrison's clashes with the powers of state politics clearly revealed that Southern nationalism and post-Civil War nostalgia overwhelmingly informed the historical consciousness of Texans at the turn of the century. George Garrison responded to it and to the realization that professional methods of research, to be of value, ultimately must be transmuted into common knowledge: in the words of historian Carl Becker, "that pattern of remembered events, whether true or false, that enlarges and enriches the collective specious present of Mr. Everyman." In allusion to the quip that history was a trick the living played on the dead, Becker wrote: "The appropriate trick for any age is not a malicious invention designed to take anyone in, but an unconscious and necessary effort on the part of 'society' to understand what it is doing in the light of what it has done and what it hopes to do." Historians by profession share in this necessary effort. "But we do not impose our version of the human story on Everyman; in the end it is rather Mr. Everyman who imposes his version on us."[31] Certainly historians of Texas found this to be true.

By the late nineteenth century it became clear that Americans in general, and Texans in particular, could not or would not relinquish their romantic worldview. Nearly every aspect of life was changing in the last two decades of the nineteenth century: urban industrialism was overtaking agrarianism; scientists and mathematicians like Henrí Poincaré were challenging the perfect order of Newtonian mechanics; the scientific method was overtaking literary methods of writing history; and the patricians, who had been the elite of American history writers, were displaced by the professional elite, though, in principle, they differed little from one another.

In Texas, as in the United States at large, the population reacted to the unsettling effects of war, industrialization, and threats to basic assumptions that had guided their thinking for generations by retreating into nostalgia, clinging stubbornly to the unchanging principle of moral progress, and creating myths in the guise of history. Becker suggested that all people embroider personal experience with memories of things reputed to have been said and done in past times that they have not known. It does not matter that these memories be completely true, said Becker, only that they be useful. People will hold in memory only those things that can be related to their ideas of themselves. "The history which [the individual] imaginatively recreates as an artificial extension of his personal experience will inevitably be an engaging blend of fact and fancy. . . . In part it will be true, in part false; as a whole perhaps neither true nor false."[32]

Texas history in the late nineteenth century became the province of every man and woman in a very real sense. Much of published history consisted of personal accounts and memoirs. Of the two Texas books to make the list of national best-sellers in the nineteenth century, one, Kendall's *Narrative,* was just such a work; the other, *Mr. Potter's Texas,* was fiction.[33] Many of the changes wrought by the shift from romantic to realistic paradigm were evident in the proliferation of monographs and short articles, compilations, and memorial histories. The greatest influence of scientific history manifested itself in the establishment of the Department of History at the University of Texas for training Texas historians. The work of Wooten, Garrison, and Bugbee provided a new method for would-be Texas historians to follow, but one that incorporated the romantic ideals cherished by the chivalric South, embodied in the code of the West, and embraced by Americans in their attempt to escape temporal history in a spatial one. Ultimately, professional historians in Texas found themselves constrained to join with amateurs in perpetuating the collective memory written and published in these final decades of the nineteenth century on an unprecedented scale by Texans about Texans. Texas history was still written with a purpose. In an era a little short of heroes, it provided some. Because the rugged, individualistic, pioneering Texans epitomized the American character as Americans and the world at large believed it to be, the inventors and purveyors of this image were able to export their mythistory to a receptive audience that continued to cherish it throughout the ensuing century.

7 ★ Conclusion

If, as some modern historians have charged, Texas history has resisted generational revisions, can we find an explanation in the study of nineteenth-century histories and historians for the phenomenal "shelf life" of Texas history? Best-selling Texas author T. R. Fehrenbach maintains that the "romances" of the nineteenth century "are vital to Texans' ability to see themselves as a people and to confront the future of the state," which might be logical were it not that this explanation omits so many Texans.[1] What seems prominently lacking in such reasoning is any analysis of the origins and meaning of these "romances" that would-be revisionists call popular myths. Revisionists have called for some attempt at understanding the origins of these myths and the way that previous generations looked at the past.[2]

What are the myths to which modern historians refer and to which traditionalists claim Texans owe their identity? Critical review of histories of Texas written between 1789 and 1899 reveals several recurring themes that have been identified by Texas scholars and folklorists. Familiar to most Texans is the portrayal of Texas as the Promised Land, the New Eden, "the land of beginning again." The Texas creation myth of a great nation "born in blood" centers around the Alamo and its defenders and elevates the Davy Crockett–type Texas hero, a rugged individualist who is solitary, homespun, and proficient in wilderness survival, use of firearms, and the spinning of tall tales, and triumphant without benefit of formal education. Related in many respects are a whole cluster of myths, including manifest destiny, racial superiority of the Anglo-American settlers, and the interpretation of both the Texas Revolution and the Indian wars as extensions of the apocalyptic battle between good and evil. These myths supported the concept that Protestantism was right and uniquely privileged and qualified to dictate values to all society—justifying materialism, Darwinism, and political, racial, and religious bigotry. Some of the myths that have entwined themselves in Texan historical consciousness present conflicting interpretations. One of the most prominent examples is that of the Indians, who, on the one hand, were not descended from Noah and thus possessed no soul except the one created for them by Christians or, on the other hand, were noble by virtue of their innocence of the profane and materialistic and their proximity to nature. Perhaps this dualistic tendency accounts for the difficulty of pinpointing the source of the Texas mystique: the contradiction between progress and pastoralism, piousness and iconoclasm, isolationism and community, materialism and asceticism. Also prominent is the definition of Texans as *against* the other two groups with which they share their regional history, Hispanics and Indians. In fact, Texans have tended to define themselves as against non-Texans generally. Herein lies, possibly, the most pervasive and most ironic of all myths informing Texas history, the idea that Texas is unique, "a whole other country" or "a state of mind," an exception to the mistakes and woes of the rest of the world. Therefore, by extension, Texans are unique, a distinct people, and this may provide the inclusiveness absent in other Texas "romances."

Ironically, a reading of the history of Texas from the beginning of its recognition as a region distinguished from New Spain reveals nothing really original in Texas' most cherished myths about itself. Its myths stem from Judeo-Christian myths that existed before Columbus set foot in the New World. The myth of a New World Eden and the Promised Land is the most prominent feature of the westering myth that drove Europeans to seek redemption and a second chance in the West and wealth in a northwest passage or Quivira or California. "For God, for gold, for glory" motivated not only Catholic Spaniards but also Anglo-Protestants and produced fierce competition between them two centuries before the Texas Revolution. Texas creation myth goes back to Genesis (1:26, 28) as does manifest destiny, both outgrowths of Protestantism. The portrayal of Mexicans as evil, dirty, inferior, and somehow incapable of democratic values also flows, at least in part, from Protestantism's aversion to Catholicism. The historical treatment of Indians and African Americans appears to be a variation on the same theme, racism masquerading as myth. It produces the "them against us" interpretation of the Texas Revolution, while the post–Civil War refrain seems both to derive from and contribute to the notion of Texas nationalism and exceptionalism.

Interestingly enough, revision of these myths seems to have taken place regularly in the writing of Texas' historians prior to the Civil War, primarily for two reasons. First, those who wrote about Texas reflected the cultural climate of their own times with respect to standards of proof and methods of historical writing. Second, virtually all of them had some utilitarian purpose for writing about Texas at all.

Enlightenment ideas regarding the application of "scientific method" to determine the truth about the past, the search for cause and effect, the concept of progress, the discriminating use of existing sources, and the employment of history as an instrument of political criticism and social reform influenced Spanish missionaries Juan Agustín Morfi and José Antonio Pichardo to use every source available to them to write meticulously factual histories in order to argue their respective causes. Both sought to revise existing notions about aspects of Texas history: Morfi to counter the damaging report of Bonilla, and Pichardo to clarify the ambiguities surrounding the boundary of Louisiana and Texas. Both were effusive in their description of Texas as an earthly paradise, which suited their immediate purpose of persuading Spanish authorities that Texas was worth holding on to. Although paternalistic (as one might expect of a priest), Morfi's view of the natives recognized cultural differences without condescension.

William Darby, American geographer and journalist, likewise confined his account of the Gutiérrez-Magee expedition to his dispassionate observations as a scientist and journalist. Eschewing Anglo-Spanish conflict as a cosmic clash between the forces of good and evil, Darby pointed out the self-serving motives of the filibusters. He urged his readers to recognize cultural differences between themselves and their southern neighbors, placing the event in the context of world events and universal history.

By the time serious tension began to develop between Mexico and its frontier province of Texas, romanticism had replaced rationalism as an intellectual paradigm. Romanticists viewed past ages sympathetically, going so far as to assert that primitive savagery was superior to civilized life, a notion from which the myth of the noble savage derived. This nostalgia for the past, particularly a fascination with the Middle Ages, became especially influential in the American South. The romanticists maintained that unconscious creative forces operated mysteriously in defiance of direct intellectual analysis and that these psychic influences were responsible for the development of unique cultural and national identity, referred to by Leopold von Ranke as the *Zeitgeist*.[3] Romantic history was the history of great men and was universal in the sense that great men reflected the character of the people they represented. At the same time, English literature, especially the historical romances of Sir Walter Scott, exerted great influence on American writers. Scott's storytelling heightened the effect of history with the high adventure and emotional warmth of fiction. He was, by far, the best-selling author in the United States until the Civil War, and his readers came to expect as much from their historians as from a novelist.[4] "It may be laid down as a general rule, though subject to considerable qualifications and exceptions, that history begins in Novel and ends in Essay," wrote a reviewer in 1828.[5] Further, a revival of piety swept the Western world during the early 1800s. Writing history demonstrated truth, so history became a vehicle for moral instruction. Thus, nostalgia for the distant past, consciousness of national identity, moralism, and desire for colorful, literary history affected the style and the content of Texas histories written during the second quarter of the nineteenth century.

Texas historians of the 1830s and 1840s, educated in the style of their day and sensitive to the expectations of their audience, certainly exhibited the characteristics of romanticism in their writing. Whether they were writing to advance a political cause or to realize financial gain, they first had to sell their books. Those who sought to profit from their work, to win political support for Texan independence, or to teach moral lessons tended to advance and embellish existing myths of the New Eden, manifest destiny, superiority of the white race, and the heroism of the Texan revolutionaries. Others, such as David Edward and N. Doran Maillard, whose interests were adversely affected by the Texas Revolution, or Frédéric LeClerc, a more or less detached observer, countered with more sympathetic views of Mexicans and Indians and the concept of Texans as lazy, shiftless, corrupt, and dishonorable in their dealings with Mexico. The one myth that characterized all their writing was that of Texas as a New Eden. Even the history of the Texas Revolution written by the Mexican general Vicente Filisola, while acknowledging strengths and weaknesses of both sides, lamented that Mexico had "given away the lands of a paradise."[6] The themes that dominated Texas history in the 1830s and 1840s—morality, liberty, patriotism, progress, and Providence—generally dominated historical writing in that period, and the passionate, emotional romantic writing style that characterized Texas histories generally characterized the popular style of that era.

By the 1850s, ideas about method and style of writing history began to change in general, and it began to change in Texas as well. Auguste Comte, founder of sociology, began to influence American opinions about the application of the methods of natural science to history. Critics and reviewers called for history of "the very life of the people . . . the knowledge of which can alone furnish a true picture of the age and the actual conditions of society."[7] Greater emphasis on the particular extended to research, use of original materials, and documentation of sources as well. These trends became apparent in the writing of Texas historians of that era. William Gouge and José Antonio Navarro both wrote on particular topics rather than comprehensive history. For Gouge, Texas history was useful in arguing his views on financial institutions. Navarro concentrated on revising the historical record with regard to Tejanos. Gouge regarded his work as documentary history. Navarro's articles aimed specifically at dispelling myths of manifest destiny and racism.

Henderson Yoakum, by contrast, produced another comprehensive history of Texas that tended to perpetuate romantic themes and most of the Anglo-Texan myths rooted in Protestantism and the agrarian ideal. Nevertheless, Yoakum demonstrated the influence of changing views about history, which demanded meticulous research and documentation. In this he succeeded well enough to be recognized as more thorough and faithful to sources than his predecessors were. Perhaps the fact that many of his contemporaries in Texas did not think his history quite romantic enough was testimony to the influence of new methods and style in his writing. In this sense, Yoakum was transitional, combining a romantic view of the past with more modern methods of documenting it, which would prove to have greater significance later than it did at the time he wrote. By mid-nineteenth century, then, those with personal or political interests in promoting Anglo-Texan myths viewed Texas history through the end of the Mexican War as fulfilling those myths, while others took an opposite or more neutral view. Regardless of their approach, most were primarily interested in selling their work to the reading public. In any event, Texas historians seemed to view Texas' past in a manner consistent with that of historians elsewhere during the same era, yet not with total uniformity.

If the trend toward a more detailed, scientific approach to history in the 1850s began to change the way historians viewed the past, the Civil War certainly influenced the way they viewed it, especially in the South. Following the war, the upsurge of American nationalism centered around a revival of interest in national origins and the memorialization of national heroes. Texans, smarting from Confederate defeat and military government, turned to their own revolution and the memorialization of its heroes. Even figures like Sam Houston, who had received mixed reviews, at best, before the Civil War, were elevated to the status of icons after it. Those who wrote in this vein, such as James Morphis, were well received, but those who attempted a less biased, more objective approach or who failed to show sufficient appreciation for Texas' fallen worthies met with criticism and opposition. That is not to say that revision did not take place. Several historians of the 1870s and 1880s introduced new ways of looking at Texas history. Reuben Potter reexamined former accounts of the battle of the Alamo and attacked myths of Texan triumph based on the ideas of Providence and racial superiority. Whereas William Gouge in the 1850s had seen the financial history of Texas as United States history in microcosm, Potter saw Texas history in terms of its impact on the United States and the world. Hubert Howe Bancroft took his view of Texas' past a few steps further and treated Texas in a larger historical and geographical context. Neither Potter nor Bancroft was very well received in

Texas. Potter went largely unnoticed, and Bancroft was openly criticized for his editorial methods, which distracted attention from the content of his work. Perhaps noteworthy as well was the fact that Potter, Bancroft, and most of the other historians of the post–Civil War decades were not Texas or even Southern natives. By the 1890s, most, if not all, Texas historians were Texans.

Ironically, even as the University of Texas officially established a Department of History, Texas history began to be dominated by Gilded Age nostalgia and became very much the province of the amateur historian. Efforts of professionally trained historian George P. Garrison to collect and preserve original sources of Texas history, despite his scholarly motivations, served to encourage the popular appetite for memoirs, reminiscences, and memorials. As industrialization increased, Yoakum's agrarian ideal held even greater appeal for Texans of the late nineteenth century than it had for its contemporaries. Other facets of the Protestant myth, such as manifest destiny and Anglo-Saxon racial superiority, were reinvigorated as well. School histories of the 1890s were more passionately romantic and moralistic than histories of the romantic era had been. Faced with a rapidly changing and uncertain world, influential writers and publishers such as Dudley Wooten and John Henry Brown elevated Texas myth to the status of "history." Professional historians such as George Garrison and Lester Bugbee may have attempted to counter the trend with scholarly work, but they were vastly outnumbered, overshadowed, and politically outmaneuvered. The revolutionary generation was aging and dying out, and many with power and influence, like Governor Oran M. Roberts and John Henry Brown, used them to ensure the lionization of their memory and deeds. Texas history at the end of the nineteenth century was more popular, more democratic, and more steeped in myth than it had ever been.

Thus, the "romances of the nineteenth century" that have so resisted revision in the twentieth century are less a product of the romantic era of the 1830s and 1840s than of the late nineteenth century, and less a product of historical paradigm than of the post–Civil War Texas psyche. Because Texas historians of the nineteenth century were motivated by primarily personal agendas, whether promotional, political, or ideological, early histories of Texas did not always conform to the prevailing philosophy of history, but the influence of the intellectual climate was nevertheless discernible.

The Civil War, however, seemed to arrest the development of Texas history. In the face of disillusioning and humiliating defeat and the erosion of the agrarian ideal at a time of rapid industrialization, Texans reached back to a pre–Civil War paradigm in an effort to create and preserve for themselves a unique identity, a world apart. They saw history as a way to redeem Texas from the debacle of the Lost Cause, as something they could use as a means of positively confronting the future. Significantly, perhaps, Texas historians by the latter decades of the nineteenth century were predominantly Texans rather than visitors or transplants, as in earlier years, and it was with this myth of their exceptionalism that Texans faced the twentieth century.

In a final twist of irony, we realize that even this most self-defining idea is myth, for Texans share it with generations of Americans who immigrated to the New World in the belief that they were escaping the flaws of human nature that troubled the society and culture of the Old World. We realize that the "Texas myth" is, in fact, not unique at all. It follows, in a direct line, age-old Judeo-Christian myths, especially the westering myth, and the myth of American exceptionalism.[8] In spite of the frequently noted clash of cultures, many of its facets are shared by Spanish and Anglo Texans. It is possibly the overwhelming desire—material, psychological, and emotional—to hold on to this concept of uniqueness that has made Texas history so resistant to revision.

Notes

INTRODUCTION

1. Walter L. Buenger and Robert A. Calvert, eds., *Texas through Time: Evolving Interpretations,* xiii.

2. C. Vann Woodward, *Thinking Back: The Perils of Writing History,* chap. 1.

3. Buenger and Calvert, *Texas through Time,* xi.

4. Joe B. Frantz, "Lone Star Mystique," *American West* 5 (May 1968): 9.

5. Juan Agustín Morfi, *History of Texas, 1673–1779,* vol. 1, trans. Carlos Eduardo Castañeda, 48–49.

6. Fray José Antonio Pichardo, *Pichardo's Treatise on the Limits of Louisiana and Texas,* vol. 2, trans. and ed. Charles W. Hackett, xiv.

7. William Kennedy, *Texas: The Rise, Progress, and Prospects of the Republic of Texas, in One Volume,* xix.

8. The phrase, "to improve the accuracy of impression," came from "The Romance of History," a review of *England,* by Henry Neele, *Edinburgh Review* 47 (May 1828): 331–67. In its original context, it referred to characteristics of romantic history in general and not specifically to Yoakum.

9. Henderson Yoakum to Martin Van Buren, 6 June 1845, Martin Van Buren Papers, Presidential Papers Microfilm, Library of Congress Series 2, reel 30.

10. Quoted in Bowen C. Tatum Jr., "A Texas Patriot," *Texas Bar Journal* 53 (Sept. 1970): 722.

11. Dudley G. Wooten, ed, *A Comprehensive History of Texas, 1685 to 1897,* vol. 1, v; C. W. Raines, review of *A Comprehensive History of Texas,* by Dudley G. Wooten, *Quarterly of the Texas State Historical Association* 2 (July 1898): 90–91; Z. T. Fulmore, *The History and Geography of Texas as Told in County Names,* 151; Herbert Gambrell, "Scholars of the Past Find Our History a Rich Field," *Dallas Times Herald,* 7 Oct. 1945; Eugene C. Barker, "Professor Barker Considers Growth of Our Historians," *Dallas Morning News,* 7 Oct. 1945.

12. R. G. Collingwood, *The Idea of History,* 33.

13. New York *Turf, Field, and Farm,* quoted in *Dallas Weekly Herald,* 12 Dec. 1874; *Dallas Weekly Herald,* 9 Jan. 1875.

14. Robert A. Calvert, introduction to *A Texas Scrapbook. Made up of the History, Biography, and Miscellany of Texas and Its People,* compiled by D. W. C. Baker, xxii.

15. Raines, review of *Comprehensive History of Texas,* 89.

16. Quoted in John H. Jenkins, *Basic Texas Books,* 56.

17. Larry McMurtry, *In a Narrow Grave: Essays on Texas,* 38; Buenger and Calvert, *Texas through Time,* xi.

I. PROLOGUE

1. Morfi, *History of Texas,* vol. 1, 48.

2. Carlos Eduardo Castañeda, "Biographical Introduction," in Morfi, *History of Texas,* vol. 1, 16.

3. Ibid., 19, 23–25.

4. A translation by Elizabeth Howard West of Antonio Bonilla's *Breve Compendio de la Historia de Texas* appeared in the *Quarterly of the Texas Historical Association* 8 (July 1904): 3–78.

5. Castañeda, "Biographical Introduction," 26.

6. Morfi, *History of Texas,* vol. 1, 48–49.

7. See Edmundo O'Gorman, *The Invention of America: An Inquiry into the Historical Nature of the New World and Meaning of Its History;* also Harry Bernstein, "Some Inter-American Aspects of the Enlightenment," in *Latin America and the Enlightenment,* ed. Arthur P. Whitaker, 2d ed. (Ithaca, N.Y.: Cornell University Press), 53–55; Henry Nash Smith, *Virgin Land: The American West as Symbol and Myth,* 139, 293–98; and R. W. B. Lewis, *The American Adam: Innocence, Tragedy, and Tradition in the Nineteenth Century,* 5.

8. Morfi, *History of Texas,* vol. 1, 79–92.

9. Ibid., 161.

10. For a detailed explanation of the inspection and report of Revera and Morfi's refutation of it, see Morfi, *History of Texas,* vol. 2, 244–74.

11. Pichardo, *Treatise,* vol. 1, passim; *Hubert Howe Bancroft, North Mexican States and Texas, 1531–1800,* 631–32.

12. Castañeda, "Biographical Introduction," 33–34.

13. Pichardo, *Treatise,* vol. 1, 4. Pichardo made it clear in his introduction that the entrance of the United States into the territorial matters concerning the region prompted the necessity for a concise history of the boundary question; see also Charles W. Hackett's comments, ibid., xiv.

14. Ron Tyler et al., eds., *The New Handbook of Texas,* vol. 5, 189. Some discrepancy exists with regard to Pichardo's birth date. Charles W. Hackett noted that according to the Mexican bibliographer Medina, Pichardo was born in 1732. See Pichardo, *Treatise,* vol. 1, xviii.

15. Luis Monguío, "Las Luces and the Enlightenment in Spanish America," in *The Ibero-American Enlightenment,* ed. A. Owen Aldridge (Urbana: University of Illinois Press, 1971), 216–17; Pichardo, *Treatise,* vol. 1, xviii; Tyler et al., *New Handbook of Texas,* vol. 5, 188–89; vol. 6, 195.

16. For this reason Carlos E. Castañeda asserted that Pichardo's *Treatise* was not in fact a history but an argumentative brief with definite limitations as a history of Spanish Texas. Morfi, *History of Texas,* vol. 1, 292.

17. Pichardo, *Treatise,* vol. 1, 292; quotes, 27, 38.

18. Ibid., xix.

19. Ibid., first quote, vol. 4, ix–x; second quote, vol. 4, 441–42.

20. Ibid., vol. 1, 4.

21. Ibid., xx, 390.

22. Ibid., vol. 2, xiv.

23. Arthur P. Whitaker, ed., introduction to *Latin America and the Enlightenment,* xiii.

2. TEXAS HISTORIANS AND THE ROMANTIC REVOLUTION

1. Helmut Lehman-Haupt, *The Book in America: A History of the Making and Selling of Books in the United States,* 177, 123–24.

2. See, for example, Thomas W. Streeter, *Bibliography of Texas, 1795–1845;* C. W. Raines, *A Bibliography of Texas;* John H. Jenkins, *Texas History: One Thousand Rare Books, with Additional Sections on Texas Maps, Photographs, and Manuscripts, and a Selection on the Mexican War;* Antonio Palau y Dulcet, *Manuel del Librero Hispano-Americano,* contains hundreds of imprints relating specifically to Texas among its nearly four hundred thousand entries.

3. George N. Callcott, *History in the United States 1800–1860: Its Practice and Purpose,* provides a thoroughly detailed discussion of the characteristics of the romantic historian.

4. Edward Pessen, *Jacksonian America: Society, Personality, and Politics,* 18, and passim;*Michael Kammen, Spheres of Liberty: Changing Perceptions of Liberty in American Culture,* 74.

5. Sister (Paul of the Cross) McGrath, *Political Nativism in Texas, 1825–1860,* 23.

6. William Darby, "Province of Texas," *Niles Weekly Register,* supplement to vol. 16 (7 Aug. 1819): 42–46.

7. Frank Luther Mott, *A History of American Magazines, 1741–1850,* vol. 1, 161–62.

8. *Dictionary of American Biography,* s.v., "Darby, William."

9. John William Tebbel, *A History of Book Publishing in the United States,* vol. 1, 121; and Mott, *History of American Magazines,* vol. 1, 268.

10. Darby, "Province of Texas," first quote, 42; second quote, 44; third quote, 45.

11. L. D. Clark, "Texas Historical Writing: A Sample of the Myth at Age 150," *American West* 23 (Jan./Feb. 1986): 80.J. P. Bryan in his introduction to Mary Austin Holley's *Mary Austin Holley: The Texas Diary, 1835–1838,* called her the first credible historian of Texas and possibly one of the best-known women in North America during the first part of the nineteenth century. See also Stephen Stagner, "Epics, Science, and the Lost Frontier: Texas Historical Writing, 1836–1936," *Western Historical Quarterly* 12 (Apr. 1981): 166, and Jenkins, *Basic Texas Books,* 242.

12. Mott, *History of American Magazines,* 1:311.

13. Rebecca Smith Lee, *Mary Austin Holley, A Biography,* 223; see also Marilyn McAdams Sibley, introduction to *Texas,* by Mary Austin Holley, n.p.n.; quote from Mary Austin Holley, *Texas,* vi–vii.

14. Mary Austin Holley, *Letters of an Early American Traveller: Mary Austin Holley, Her Life and Her Works,* ed. Mattie Austin Hatcher, 63; Holley, *Texas,* 309.

15. "The Modern Art and Science of History," *Westminster Review* 30 (Oct. 1842): 369.

16. Holley, *Texas,* 3, v, 182; quotes, v–vi. The use of the phrase "rise of the common man," occurred frequently during the Jacksonian era. Thus, "man" is used here in the nineteenth-century context.

17. Ibid., first quote, 180; second quote, 128; third quote, 298–99.

18. Mary Austin Holley to Orville L. Holley, 24 Dec. 1831, Mary Austin Holley Papers, Center for American History, University of Texas at Austin. Holley's *Texas* repre-

sented the first book printing of a number of key documents of the revolution, including the Texas Declaration of Independence, the Constitution of the Republic of Texas, and Travis's famous victory-or-death letter from the Alamo, as well as the Mexican Constitution of 1824 and her translation of the colonization laws.

19. Holley, *Texas,* 9.

20. Mary Austin Holley to Orville L. Holley, 24 Dec. 1831, Holley Papers.

21. Mary Austin Holley to Harriette, 22 Apr. 1833; Mary Austin Holley to Harriette, 19 Dec. 1833, Holley Papers.

22. Holley, *Letters of an Early American Traveller,* 97; Henry Austin to M. A. Holley, 8 Nov. 1836, Holley Papers.

23. David B. Edward, *The History of Texas; or, The Emigrant's, Farmer's, and Politician's Guide to the Character, Climate, Soil and Productions of that Country: Geographically Arranged and from Personal Observation and Experience,* ix (emphasis his).

24. Ibid., ix; Jenkins, *Basic Texas Books,* 130–40; Edward, *History of Texas,* viii.

25. Lehman-Haupt, *The Book in America,* 215–16; Tebbel, *History of Book Publishing,* 1:481–82.

26. Edward, *History of Texas,* viii. Emphasis Edward's.

27. John T. Mason to Stephen F. Austin, 5 July 1836, Austin Papers, Center for American History, University of Texas at Austin; B. T. Archer to J. T. Mason, 23 July 1836, Austin Papers; Pease quoted in Jenkins, *Basic Texas Books,* 140; Iva M. Bryant, "David Barnett Edward, Notes on His Life," Edward Family Papers, 1838–1936, Center for American History, University of Texas at Austin.

28. Raines, *Bibliography of Texas,* 74.

29. Edward, *History of Texas,* xii.

30. Ibid., quote, 115; ix; 116 (emphasis his).

31. Ibid., 177–79; 181; 182–254.

32. The term "Indian" is used here to refer to indigenous peoples because it is the term Edward and his contemporaries used.

33. Edward, *History of Texas,* 92–93, 95, 97.

34. Ibid., 269–79; see Henry David Thoreau, "Civil Disobedience," in *Works of Henry David Thoreau,* ed. Lily Owens, 415–47.

35. Edward, *History of Texas,* first quote, 295; second quote, 299.

36. Ibid., 37–39, 41.

37. Quotes, ibid., vii. Certain of his Texas critics accused Edward, with some justification, of plagiarizing Mary Austin Holley's work. He copied entire sentences verbatim from Holley's 1833 book and, according to John H. Jenkins, often used available sources without giving credit. Jenkins, *Basic Texas Books,* 139; Raines, *Bibliography of Texas,* 74.

38. Family Memorial, Edward Family Papers.

39. Amelia W. Williams and Eugene C. Barker, eds., *The Writings of Sam Houston, 1813–1863,* 2:203; see also Jenkins, *Basic Texas Books,* 403–6, and Tyler et al., *New Handbook of Texas,* vol. 4, 991; Chester Newell to Samuel M. Williams, 19 Sept. 1838, Alexander Dienst Papers, Center for American History, University of Texas at Austin.

40. Chester B. Newell, *History of the Revolution in Texas, Particularly of the War of 1835 & '36, together with the Latest Geographical, Topographical, and Statistical Accounts of the Country, from the Most Authentic Sources,* n.p.n.d.

41. Ibid., 3–11.

42. Ibid., "Preface," 13.

43. Quote, Newell, *History,* 14; Chester Newell to Samuel May Williams, 19 Sept. 1838, Dienst Papers.

44. Newell, *History,* 14–15, 23–24; 35; 189–90; 75.

45. Ibid., 75, 99.

46. Newell to Williams, 19 Sept. 1838, Dienst Papers; The *Dublin Review* never mentioned the merit of Newell's book as history except to dub it "partisan." Review of *History of the Revolution in Texas,* by the Rev. Chester Newel [*sic*], *Dublin Review* 12 (Dec. 1838): 663.

47. Lehman-Haupt, *The Book in America,* 129.

48. James L. Shepherd III, translator's preface to Frédéric LeClerc, *Texas and Its Revolution,* trans. James L. Shepherd III, xii; see also LeClerc, *Texas and Its Revolution,* 17. The first publication in book form was Frédéric LeClerc, *Le Texas et sa revolution.*

49. The second quarter of the nineteenth century was known as "the golden age of periodicals." During this time, the number of periodicals other than newspapers grew from less than a hundred in 1825 to about six hundred by 1850. Frank Luther Mott, in *History of American Magazines,* estimated that as many as four or five thousand were published in America within those twenty-five years, 1:341–42; Frederick [*sic*] LeClerc, "Texas and Its Revolution," *Southern Literary Messenger* 7 (May/June 1841): 398–421. The translator of this edition was identified by the journal's editor only as "a Gentleman of Philadelphia." Tyler et al., *New Handbook of Texas,* 4:136.

50. LeClerc, *Texas and Its Revolution,* 54–61: quote, 54; quote, 61; quote, 67.

51. Ibid., 68.

52. Ibid., 72–80; quote, 108; 86–87.

53. Ibid., 96; quote, 121.

54. Tyler et al., *New Handbook of Texas,* vol. 4, 136.

55. Edward Stiff, *The Texan Emigrant: Being a Narration of the Adventures of the Author in Texas, and a Description of the Soil, Climate, Productions, Minerals, Towns, Bays, Harbors, Rivers, Institutions, and Manners and Customs of the Inhabitants of That Country; together with the Principal Incidents of Fifteen Years Revolution in Mexico: and Embracing a Condensed Statement of Interesting Events in Texas, from the First European Settlement in 1692, down to the Year 1840,* iii–iv.

56. Jenkins, *Basic Texas Books,* 524; Tony E. Duty, introduction to *Texan Emigrant,* by Edward Stiff, n.p.n.; Houston *Telegraph and Texas Register,* 2 Mar. 1842.

57. Stiff, *Texan Emigrant,* 13–14.

58. Ibid., iv.

59. Ibid., 103.

60. Ibid., 12.

61. Tebbel, *History of Book Publishing,* vol. 1, 237; Lehman-Haupt, *The Book in America,* 259.

62. Detlef Dunt, *Reise nach Texas, nebst Nachrichten von diesem Lande: fuer Deutsche, welche nach Amerika zu gehen beabsichtigen;* Amos Andrew Parker, *A Trip to the West and Texas, Comprising a Journey of Eight Thousand Miles, through New York, Michigan, Illinois, Missouri, Louisiana and Texas, in the Autumn and Winter of 1834–5, Interspersed with Anecdotes, Incidents and Observations;* and *A Visit to Texas, Being the Journal of a Traveller through Those Parts Most Interesting to American Settlers, with Descriptions of the Scenery, &C., &C.;* L. Hartmann and Millard, *Le Texas, ou notice historique sur le Champ d'Asile, comprenant tout ce qui s'est passe depuis la formation jusqu'a la dissolution de cette colonie, les causes qui l'ont amenee, et la liste de tous les colons Français, avec des renseignemens utiles a*

leurs familles, et le plan du champ; Robert M. Coleman, *Houston Displayed; Or, Who Won the Battle of San Jacinto? By a Farmer in the Army.*

63. "History," *American Quarterly Review* 5 (Mar. 1829): 89.

3. TEXAS HISTORIANS AND THE RISE OF THE LONE STAR

1. Herbert Pickens Gambrell, *Mirabeau Buonaparte Lamar, Troubadour and Crusader,* 19–54.

2. Kennedy, *Texas,* xix.

3. *Dictionary of National Biography;* Tyler et al., *New Handbook of Texas,* vol. 3, 1069; Kennedy, *Texas,* xx, xxiii.

4. William Kennedy to Lord Aberdeen, 20 Oct. 1841, in "British Correspondence concerning Texas," *Quarterly of the Texas State Historical Association* 15 (Jan. 1912): 246–47; William Kennedy to Lord Aberdeen, 20 Apr. 1842, in "British Correspondence concerning Texas," 264–65; Kennedy and others, including William Pringle and Henri Castro, entered into a colonization contract in February 1842 to settle six hundred families in Texas, but nothing ever came of it.

5. Kennedy, *Texas,* xxxix; xli; William Kennedy to M[irabeau] B[uonaparte] L[amar], 20 Sept. 1839, Mirabeau B. Lamar Papers, Texas State Library, Archives Division.

6. Review of *The Rise, Progress, and Prospects of the Republic of Texas,* by William Kennedy, *New York Review* 9 (July 1841): 188, 208. Such a review would have had an impact in the United States. The *New York Review* was highly respected, widely distributed, and outranked all other reviews of the period in variety and interest. See Mott, *History of American Magazines,* vol. 1, 367, 669–71.

7. Thrall and Barker quoted in Jenkins, *Basic Texas Books,* 311; Frank Brown, "Annals of Travis County, and of the City of Austin: From the Earliest Times to the Close of 1875," undated typescript, 2:22, Texas State Library, Archives Division.

8. Kennedy, *Texas,* 196; 200.

9. Ibid., 258.

10. Ibid., 267; 320; 515; 565.

11. Ibid., 517; 526–27.

12. Ibid., 557.

13. See Stagner, "Epics, Science," 166; quote from letter by William Kennedy to Anson Jones in *Memoranda and Official Correspondence Relating to the Republic of Texas, Its History and Annexation,* 358.

14. Tyler et al., *New Handbook of Texas,* vol. 2, 1071.

15. Henry Stuart Foote, *Texas and the Texans; or, The Advance of the Anglo-Americans to the South-West; Including a History of Leading Events in Mexico, from the Conquest by Fernando Cortes to the Termination of the Texas Revolution,* vol. 1, iii; Ashbel Smith to Henry S. Foote, 11 Mar. 1839, Ashbel Smith Papers, Center for American History, University of Texas at Austin; T. J. Green to M. B. Lamar, 14 Aug. 1839, Lamar Papers; also Charles Adams Gulick Jr. and Katherine Elliott, eds., *The Papers of Mirabeau Buonaparte Lamar,* vol. 3, 66; vol. 2, 509, 542, 547; M. Hunt to M. B. Lamar, 5 June 1839, Lamar Papers.

16. Foote, *Texas and the Texans,* vol. 2, 15–19, 164–65, 261; quote, 274–75, 276; in Williams and Barker, *Writings of Sam Houston,* vol. 2, 395.

17. Foote, *Texas and the Texans,* vol. 1, 13–14.

18. Ibid., 15; Tyler et al., *New Handbook of Texas,* vol. 2, 1070.

19. Foote, *Texas and the Texans,* vol. 1, 148–49, 291–98; vol. 2, 272–81; quote, vol. 2, 262–63.

20. Ibid., vol. 2, 262, 275; review of *Texas and the Texans . . . ,* by Henry Stuart Foote, *New York Review* 9 (July 1841): 208.

21. [A. B. Lawrence], *Texas in 1840, or the Emigrant's Guide to the New Republic; Being the Result of Observation, Enquiry and Travel in That Beautiful Country, by an Emigrant, Late of the United States;* [A. B. Lawrence], *A History of Texas, or the Emigrant's Guide to the New Republic, by a Resident Emigrant, Late from the United States,* same printing as the original with new cancel title added.

22. [Lawrence], *A History of Texas,* xiv.

23. William S. Red, ed., "[W. Y.] Allen's Reminiscences of Texas, 1838–1842," *Southwestern Historical Quarterly* 17 (Jan. 1913): 298n. 2; and *New York Review* 9 (July 1841): 208.

24. Lawrence, *A History of Texas,* xvi; xviii.

25. Jenkins, *Basic Texas Books,* 363.

26. Clarence R. Wharton, *History of Fort Bend County,* 103.

27. Nicholas Doran Maillard, *The History of the Republic of Texas, from the Discovery of the Country to the Present Time; and the Cause of Her Separation from the Republic of Mexico,* iii; Tyler et al., *New Handbook of Texas,* vol. 4, 468; Wharton, *History of Fort Bend County,* 1–3. The significance of the Maillard-Riddell relationship is likely to remain purely speculative since the 1840 Texas census includes the name of Doran Maillard in Fort Bend County but no reference at all to Riddell.

28. Wharton, *History of Fort Bend County,* 105–6. According to Wharton, in April 1837 the Mexican Congress proposed the issue of a new series of bonds payable in 1866 and secured by land warrants in the departments of Texas, New Mexico, and California. This proposal was presented to bondholders by the Mexican agent in London (identified only as de Yturbide). After two years the deal was closed, and the new bonds and land warrants were issued.

29. Maillard, *History of the Republic of Texas,* iv, xii.

30. Ibid., xii.

31. Ibid., 178; quote, v; Review of *The History of [the Republic of] Texas,* by N. D. Maillard, *Monthly Review* 157 (1842): 174.

32. Arthur Ikin to Anson Jones, 15 Mar. 1842, and Ashbel Smith to Anson Jones, 17 May 1842, *Diplomatic Correspondence of the Republic of Texas,* pt. 3, ed. George P. Garrison, vol. 2, pt. 2 of *Annual Report of the American Historical Association for the Year 1908* (Washington, D.C.: GPO, 1911), 951, 957.

33. *Dictionary of American Biography,* s.v., "Niles, John M."; John M. Niles, *History of South America and Mexico; Comprising Their Discovery, Geography, Politics, Commerce and Revolutions. To Which is Annexed, a Geographical and Historical View of Texas, with a Detailed Account of the Texian Revolution and War,* by Hon. L. T. Pease, vol. 1, iv.

34. Niles, *History,* vol. 1, 225, 252–53.

35. Ibid., 364–65.

36. Arthur Ikin, *Texas: Its History, Topography, Agriculture, Commerce, and General Statistics. To Which is Added, a Copy of the Treaty of Commerce Entered into by the Republic of Texas and Great Britain. Designed for the Use of the British Merchant, and As a Guide to Emigrants;* Mathilda Charlotte (Jesse) Fraser Houstoun, *Texas and the Gulf of Mexico; Or, Yachting in the New World;* Prince Carl of Solms-Braunfels, *Texas; Geschildert in Beziehung auf seine geographischen, socialen, und übrigen Verhältnisse, mit besonderem Rueksicht auf die Deutsche Colonisation ein Handbuch fuer Auswanderer nach Texas.*

37. Hermann Ehrenberg, *Texas und seine Revolution;* George Wilkins Kendall, *Narrative of the Texan and Santa Fe Expedition, Comprising a Description of a Tour through Texas, and across the Great Southwestern Prairies, the Camanche and Cayuga Hunting-Grounds, with an Account of the Sufferings from Want of Food, Losses from Hostile Indians, and Final Capture of the Texans, and Their March, as Prisoners, to the City of Mexico;* William Preston Stapp, *The Prisoners of Perote: Containing a Journal Kept by the Author, Who Was Captured by the Mexicans, at Mier, December 25, 1842, and Released from Perote, May 16, 1844.*

38. Vicente Filisola, *Representación Dirigida al Supremo Gobierno . . . en Defensa de su Honor y Aclaración de sus Operaciones como General en Gefe del Ejercito Sobre Tejas.*

39. Jenkins, *Basic Texas Books,* 162; Vicente Filisola, *Memorias para la Historia de La Guerra de Tejas,* trans. Wallace Woolsey, xvii, xxv.

40. Filisola, *Memorias,* xxv, xxxi.

41. Ibid., 8, 13, 11, 16.

42. Ibid., 21, 44–45.

43. Ibid., 52.

44. Ibid., 210, xxxvi–xxxvii.

45. Thomas Bangs Thorpe, *Our Army on the Rio Grand, Being a Short Account of the Important Events Transpiring from the Time of the Removal of the "Army of Occupation," from Corpus Christi, to the Surrender of Matamoros . . . ,* and Samuel Chester Reid Jr., *The Scouting Expeditions of McCulloch's Texas Rangers . . . ;* Viktor Friederich Bracht, *Texas im Jahre 1848, nach mehrjährigen Beobachtungen dargestellt;* Jenkins, *Basic Texas Books,* 52.

4. PRIDE GOETH . . . BEFORE A FALL

1. Callcott, *History in the United States,* 173.

2. Rollin G. Osterweis, *Romanticism and Nationalism in the Old South,* 9.

3. Other books by Gouge include *A Short History of Paper Money and Banking in the United States* (1833), *History of the American Banking System* (1835), and *An Inquiry into the Expediency of Dispensing with Bank Agency and Bank Paper in Fiscal Concerns of the United States* (1837); "Remarks on the Texas Debt, and For the Issue of Certain Certificates of Stocks to Texas in Payment Thereof," 1 Mar. 1853, in Williams and Barker, *Writings of Sam Houston,* 5:409; Jenkins, *Basic Texas Books,* 201; Tyler et al., *New Handbook of Texas,* 3:256.

4. William M. Gouge, *The Fiscal History of Texas, Embracing An Account of its Revenues, Debts, and Currency, from the Commencement of the Revolution in 1834 to 1851–52 with Remarks on American Debts,* v.

5. Ibid., iv; Review of Lectures on the History of France, by Sir James Stephen, *North American Review* 75 (July 1852): 265.

6. Gouge, *Fiscal History of Texas,* 106–11; quote, 111.

7. Garrison quoted in Jenkins, *Basic Texas Books,* 202; Review of *The Fiscal History of Texas,* by William M. Gouge, *DeBow's Review* 14 (Apr. 1853): 380.

8. Jenkins, *Basic Texas Books,* 202.

9. David R. McDonald and Timothy M. Matovina, eds., *Defending Mexican Valor in Texas: José Antonio Navarro's Historical Writings, 1853–1857,* 23; quote, 63.

10. McDonald and Matovina, *Defending Mexican Valor,* first quote, 58; second quote, 44; third quote, 62.

11. Herbert H. Lang, "19th Century Historians of the Gulf States," 256. Edwin Anderson Alderman et al., eds. and comps., *Library of Southern Literature,* 15:486, say that Yoakum contributed to numerous periodicals in addition to his *History of Texas,* but they do not enumerate and none, other than excerpts from the *History,* could be found; S. W. Geiser, "Men of Science in Texas, 1820–1880," *Field and Laboratory* 27 (July 1959): 163–256, included Yoakum apparently because he was Smithsonian meteorological observer at Huntsville 1849–51; Thomas P. Yoakum, "Henderson Yoakum, Texas Historian," *Frontier Times* 27 (July 1950): 289; quote from the Huntsville *Bench and Bar,* 28 Apr. 1857, 292.

12. Lang, "19th Century Historians," 257; Carroll Van West, "Democratic Ideology and the Antebellum Historian: The Case of Henderson Yoakum," *Journal of the Early Republic* 3 (fall 1983): 320, 339.

13. Ibid., 320–21, 324; Yoakum to Martin Van Buren, 6 June 1845, Van Buren Papers.

14. Van West, "Democratic Ideology," 329; Henderson Yoakum to Martin Van Buren, 6 June 1845, Van Buren Papers.

15. Quote, Henderson King Yoakum, *History of Texas from Its First Settlement in 1865 to Its Annexation to the United States in 1846,* 1:208; 110; last quote, 2:151.

16. Yoakum, *History of Texas,* 1:403; Lang, "19th Century Historians," 280–81.

17. Yoakum, *History of Texas,* 1:282–90; Lang, "19th Century Historians," 278.

18. Yoakum, *History of Texas,* 1:209, 304–5.

19. Henderson Yoakum to T. J. Rusk, 2 June 1853, Thomas Jefferson Rusk Papers, Center for American History, University of Texas at Austin. Carroll Van West, "Democratic Ideology," 335, suggested that he probably began work in 1849; second quote, Henderson Yoakum to Dear General [Houston], 27 Jan. 1854, W. E. Pritchett Papers, Dallas Historical Society, Hall of State, Dallas, Texas.

20. Yoakum, *History of Texas,* 2:145 n.

21. *Dallas Herald* quoted in Tatum, "A Texas Patriot," 222; *The Texas Almanac, for 1857, with Statistics, Historical and Biographical Sketches, &c., Relating to Texas,* 142; Walter Moore, ed., *The Texas Almanac 1857–1873, A Compendium of Texas History,* 27.

22. Ashbel Smith to Hon. C. Anson Jones, 11 Nov. 1878, Smith Papers; P. W. Gray to Col. H. Yoakum, 18 Feb. 1856, Henderson King Yoakum Papers, Center for American History, University of Texas at Austin; J. D. B. DeBow, ed., "Texas—A Province, Republic, and State," *DeBow's Review* 23 (Sept. 1857): 239; "Literary Notices," *Harper's New Monthly Magazine* 14 (Jan. 1857): 265; Review of *History of Texas from Its Earliest Settlement . . . ,* by Henderson K. Yoakum, *Putnam's Monthly* 9 (Jan. 1857): 99.

23. Hubert Howe Bancroft, *History of the North Mexican States and Texas, 1801–1889,* vol. 16 of *The Works of Hubert Howe Bancroft,* 384; Wooten, *Comprehensive History of Texas,* 1:xiii, xxiii, v; Raines, review of *Comprehensive History of Texas,* 90–91; Fulmore, *History and Geography of Texas,* 151; Herbert Gambrell, "Scholars of the Past Find Our History a Rich Field," *Dallas Times Herald,* 7 Oct. 1945; Eugene C. Barker, "Professor Barker Considers Growth of Our Historians," *Dallas Morning News,* 7 Oct. 1945.

24. Yoakum, *History of Texas,* vol. 1, 3.

25. Ibid., 1:277–78; Henderson Yoakum to Martin Van Buren, 6 June 1845, Van Buren Papers; William H. McNeill, "Mythistory or Truth, Myth, History, and Historians," *American Historical Review* 91 (Feb. 1986): 5–6, wrote of the historian's task as putting the facts of the past together in a pattern that is understandable, credible, and useful to people. In the process, he observed, historians find themselves perpetually tempted to blend history and ideology. The product McNeill dubbed "mythistory."

5. LOST CAUSE

1. Quoted in Michael D. Kraus and David D. Joyce, *The Writing of American History*, 139; *Historical Magazine* 10 (May 1866): 166–67.

2. Kraus and Joyce, *Writing of American History*, 164.

3. Ibid., 145.

4. Ibid., 144; David Van Tassel, *Recording America's Past; An Interpretation of the Development of Historical Studies in America, 1607–1884*, 126–27.

5. Harry Elmer Barnes, *A History of Historical Writing*, 231.

6. Tyler et al., *New Handbook of Texas*, vol. 4, 842.

7. *Dallas Daily Herald*, 14 June 1874; James M. Morphis, *History of Texas from Its Discovery and Settlement, with a Description of its Principal Cities and Counties, and the Agricultural, Mineral, and Material Resources of the State*, iii, iv, viii.

8. Ibid., 454, 463.

9. New York *Turf, Field, and Farm* quoted in *Dallas Weekly Herald*, 12 Dec. 1874; *Dallas Weekly Herald*, 9 Jan. 1875.

10. Calvert, introduction to *Texas Scrapbook*, x.

11. Calvert uses 1864 as the year of Baker's election based on John P. G. McKenzie's article "DeWitt Clinton Baker School (a brief history thereof)," John P. G. McKenzie/ DeWitt Baker School, AF Public Schools Junior High (typescript), Center for American History, University of Texas at Austin. An anonymous sketch of D. W. C. Baker in the Baker Papers, Center for American History, University of Texas at Austin, gives the date as 1854; D. W. C. Baker, *A Brief History of Texas from Its Earliest Settlement*; Calvert, introduction to *Texas Scrapbook*, xiii.

12. In *Romanticism and Nationalism in the Old South*, 173–83, 198–99, Osterweis argued convincingly that literature—books, pamphlets, magazines, newspapers—had been responsible for spreading the romantic ideals that manifested themselves in the South as the cult of chivalry and contributed significantly to the growth of Southern nationalism. By the end of the 1850s, Osterweis contended, the idea of Southern nationalism had begun to catch hold in the Gulf South. Texas' imperialistic ideas before the Civil War soon fused with the drive for Southern nationalism.

13. As per letters from A. S. Barnes to DeWitt Clinton Baker, 19 Oct., 4 Nov., and 23 Dec. 1874, and 5 Jan., 5 Mar., and 19 Mar. 1875, Baker Papers.

14. Quote, D. W. C. Baker, comp., *A Texas Scrapbook. Made Up of the History, Biography, and Miscellany of Texas and Its People*, 5; Jenkins, *Basic Texas Books*, 10; Raines, *Bibliography of Texas*, 18; Calvert, introduction to *Texas Scrapbook*, xxii.

15. Homer S. Thrall, *A History of Texas, from the Earliest Settlements to the Year 1885. With an Appendix Containing the Constitution of the State of Texas, Adopted November, 1875, and the Amendments of 1883. For Use in Schools, and for General Readers;* other books by Thrall were *A Pictorial History of Texas from the Earliest Visits of European Adventurers, to A.D. 1879, The People's Illustrated Almanac, Texas Hand-book, and Immigrants' Guide . . . ,* and *A Brief History of Methodism in Texas*.

16. Thrall, *History of Texas*, 3.

17. Ibid., 53. Thrall noted that a few Africans had been smuggled into Texas, and there was some apprehension that the traffic might become extensive. The convention at San Felipe in 1833 denounced this trade. He further stated that, despite the prohibitions of 1829 and 1830 against the introduction of slavery, colonists continued to bring Negro

servants, passing them through the Custom House at New Orleans. Masters, also, entered into peonage contracts with their slaves, which the Mexican government recognized as binding.

18. Thrall, *Pictorial History of Texas*, iv.

19. Temple Lea Houston, "Thrall's *History of Texas*," *Galveston News*, 28 Sept. 1880.

20. Reuben M. Potter to M. A. Bryan, 15 Aug. 1883, Reuben Marmaduke Potter Papers, Center for American History, University of Texas at Austin.

21. Reuben M. Potter, *The Fall of the Alamo: A Reminiscence of the Texas Revolution.*

22. Reuben M. Potter, "The Fall of the Alamo," *Magazine of American History* 2 (Jan. 1878): 1–3, 14, 19.

23. Reuben M. Potter, "The Texas Revolution: Distinguished Mexicans Who Took Part in the Revolution of Texas, With Glances at Its Early Events," *Magazine of American History* 2 (Oct. 1878): 577–603. Navarro undoubtedly had some influence on Potter, who had served as his interpreter in the Senate.

24. First quote, Reuben M. Potter, "Texas Admitted to the Union," *Magazine of American History* 10 (Aug. 1883): 100; second quote, Reuben M. Potter, "The Battle of San Jacinto," *Magazine of American History* 4 (May 1880): 348.

25. Reuben M. Potter, "A Prophetic Article Published in the *Galveston Civilian* in 1845"; quote, Potter, "The Battle of San Jacinto," 349.

26. Adele B. Looscan to Charles Ramsdell, 4 Apr. 1916, Texas State Historical Association Records, Correspondence, Center for American History, University of Texas at Austin.

6. EVERY TEXAN AN HISTORIAN

1. Numerous scholars have put forth this argument, including Rollin G. Osterweis, Wilbur Cash, Robert Penn Warren, and David M. Potter. See James Marten, *Texas Divided*, 178–79.

2. Historian David D. Van Tassel marked the founding of the American Historical Association in 1884 as the climax of an epoch in American historiography. It was from that point, he contended, that one of the major shifts in American history writing occurred: the shift in dominance from the amateur to professional historian. Van Tassel, *Recording America's Past*, 171.

3. Dorothy Ross, "Historical Consciousness in the Nineteenth Century," *American Historical Review* 89 (Oct. 1984): 921. Ross's article, pp. 909–28, discusses this thesis in depth, arguing that neither the American public nor American intellectuals ever fully accepted European historicism; David D. Van Tassel, "From Learned Society to Professional Organization: The American Historical Association, 1884–1900," *American Historical Review* 89 (Oct. 1984): 948.

4. John Higham, *History, Professional Scholarship in America*, 94.

5. Michael Kammen, *Mystic Chords of Memory: The Transformation of Tradition in American Culture*, 295–96. Kammen has defined nostalgia as a concept that tends to deny the notion that progress or change is necessarily for the better. He observed further that it is especially likely to occur in response to dramatic changes, such as revolution or civil war, rapid industrialization, or the crumbling of a venerated value system. All of those phenomena, he pointed out, were present in the United States between 1860 and 1917.

6. Lehman-Haupt, *The Book in America,* 123, 199, 321; see appendices of best-sellers and better-sellers in Frank Luther Mott, *Golden Multitudes: The Story of Best Sellers in the United States,* 303–29.

7. Hubert Howe Bancroft, *Literary Industries,* vol. 39 of *The Works of Hubert Howe Bancroft,* 529–93, 601.

8. Ibid., 593, 600.

9. John Walton Caughey, *Hubert Howe Bancroft, Historian of the West,* is the only complete account of Bancroft's life and work.

10. Actually, 1521–1889, as the first chapter covers the years 1521–30.

11. According to Jenkins, *Basic Texas Books,* 13, the list of "Authorities Quoted" in Bancroft's first volume alone contained over twelve hundred printed works, not including manuscripts.

12. Bancroft, *Literary Industries,* 177, 599–617, and passim; Hubert Howe Bancroft, "History Writing," *Essays and Miscellany,* vol. 38 of *The Works of Hubert Howe Bancroft,* 75–112.

13. Raines, *A Bibliography of Texas,* 21: "Book Reviews and Notices," *Quarterly of the Texas State Historical Association* 8 (July 1904): 88, 89.

14. David Van Tassell, *Recording America's Past,* 168.

15. Walter F. McCaleb, review of *A Comprehensive History of Texas,* ed. Dudley G. Wooten, *The Dial* 29 (Sept. 1900): 122–24; Raines, review of *A Comprehensive History of Texas,* 87, 89.

16. Ibid., 91. This is an interesting distinction. Two years earlier Raines had declared Bancroft's *History* the one indispensable work on Texas history, but Bancroft, of course, was not a Texan.

17. Ibid., 91, 93.

18. Andrew Jackson Sowell, *Rangers and Pioneers of Texas, with a Concise Account of the Early Settlements, Hardships, Massacres, Battles, and Wars by Which Texas Was Rescued from the Rule of the Savage and Consecrated to the Empire of Civilization;* John Wesley Wilbarger, *Indian Depredations in Texas: Reliable Accounts of Battles, Wars, Adventures, Forays, Murders, Massacres, Etc., Etc., together with Biographical Sketches of Many of the Most Noted Indian Fighters and Frontiersmen of Texas.*

19. Will S. James, *27 Years a Mavrick or Life on a Texas Range.*

20. Jenkins, *Basic Texas Books,* 54; John Henry Brown, *History of Texas from 1685 to 1892,* first quote, 1:4; second quote, 3; reviews quoted in Jenkins, *Basic Texas Books,* 56.

21. Dudley G. Wooten, *A Complete History of Texas for Schools, Colleges, and General Use.*

22. M. E. M. Davis, *Under Six Flags, The Story of Texas,* v.

23. Kraus and Joyce, *Writing of American History,* 239; See John Higham, *Writing American History, Essays on Modern Scholarship,* 119.

24. Higham, *Writing American History,* 119.

25. George P. Garrison, "Scientific and Literary Historians," *Popular Science Monthly* 58 (Nov. 1900), 92; See David W. Noble, *Historians against History: The Frontier Thesis and the National Covenant in American Historical Writing since 1830,* 3. Noble hypothesizes that the concept of American deliverance from the vicissitudes of history found its final expression in Jacksonian democracy, which embraced moral progress and the beneficent power of the Union simultaneously.

26. Quote, H. Y. Benedict, "George Pierce Garrison," *Quarterly of the Texas State Historical Association* 14 (Jan. 1911): 175.

27. H. Y. Benedict, comp., *A Source Book Relating to the History of the University of Texas: Legislative, Legal, Bibliographical, and Statistical,* 406.

28. James Sutton Payne, "Texas Historiography in the Twentieth Century: A Study of Eugene C. Barker, Charles W. Ramsdell, and Walter P. Webb," 79, 70.

29. Maggie Watters to Mr. [L. G.] Bugbee, 16 June 1897; Anna J. H. Pennybacker to [L. G.] Bugbee, 2 Oct. 1897, Lester Gladstone Bugbee Papers, Center for American History, University of Texas at Austin.

30. George P. Garrison to Gov. O. M. Roberts, 15 Feb. 1897, Texas State Historical Association Records; see O. M. Roberts, "The Proper Work of the Association," *Quarterly of the Texas State Historical Association* 1 (July 1897): 3–8.

31. Carl Becker, "Everyman His Own Historian," *American Historical Review* 37 (Jan. 1932): 234–35.

32. Kammen, *Mystic Chords of Memory,* 17; quotes, Becker, "Everyman His Own Historian," 230.

33. Mott, *Golden Multitudes,* 315–29.

7. CONCLUSION

1. Quoted in Debbie Nathan, "Forget the Alamo," *Texas Monthly,* 26 Apr. 1998, 105, 126–28.

2. Buenger and Calvert, *Texas through Time,* xiii.

3. R. G. Collingwood, *The Idea of History* (Oxford: Clarendon Press, 1946), 87; Barnes, *A History of Historical Writing,* 178.

4. Review of *The Romance of History,* by Henry Neele, *Edinburgh Review* 47 (May 1828): 361–63; Review of *The Life of Napoleon Buonaparte, Emperor of the French,* by [Sir Walter Scott], *Christian Examiner* 4 (Sept. 1827): 382; Harry Hayden Clark, *Transitions in American Literary History,* 202–10; Callcott, *History in the United States,* 9; David Levin, *History as Romantic Art: Bancroft, Prescott, Motley, and Parkman,* 11.

5. Review of *The Romance of History,* 331–32.

6. Filisola, *Memorias,* 210.

7. "The Aim of History," *Biblical Repertory and Princeton Review* 29 (Apr. 1857): 214.

8. In his book *The Super-Americans* (Garden City, N.Y.: Doubleday, 1961), John Bainbridge observed, "In this country the frontier still holds a mystical fascination. According to the idealized concept, life on the frontier has always been simpler and happier, and a man could be luckier there. The so-called American Dream . . . seems to come true most often in Texas. The faults of Texas, as recorded by most visitors, are the same ones the Europeans have been taxing Americans with for 300 years. Texas is a mirror in which Americans see themselves reflected, not life-sized but bigger than life. [Texans] are the Super-Americans, making up a little civilization—the United States in microcosm" (5–6).

Bibliography

ARCHIVES AND PAPERS

Austin Papers. Center for American History, University of Texas at Austin.

Baker, D. W. C. Papers. Center for American History, University of Texas at Austin.

Bugbee, Lester Gladstone. Papers. Center for American History, University of Texas at Austin.

Dienst, Alexander. Papers. Center for American History, University of Texas at Austin.

Edward [David Barnett] Family. Papers. Center for American History, University of Texas at Austin.

Holley, Mary Austin. Papers. Center for American History, University of Texas at Austin.

Lamar, Mirabeau Buonaparte. Papers. Texas State Library, Archives Division, Austin.

Potter, Reuben Marmaduke. Papers. Center for American History, University of Texas at Austin.

Pritchett, W. E. Papers. Dallas Historical Society, Hall of State, Dallas, Texas.

Rusk, Thomas Jefferson. Papers. Center for American History, University of Texas at Austin.

Smith, Ashbel. Papers. Center for American History, University of Texas at Austin.

Texas State Historical Association. Records. Center for American History, University of Texas at Austin.

Van Buren, Martin. Papers. Series 2. Presidential Papers Microfilm. Library of Congress, Washington, D.C.

Yoakum, Henderson [King]. Papers. Center for American History, University of Texas at Austin.

BOOKS AND ARTICLES

"The Aim of History." *Biblical Repertory and Princeton Review* 29 (April 1857): 212–33.

Alderman, Edwin Anderson, Joel Chandler Harris, Charles William Kent, and Lucien Lamar Knight, eds. and comps. *Library of Southern Literature.* Vol. 15. New Orleans: Martin and Hoyt, 1910.

Aldridge, A. Owen, ed. *The Ibero-American Enlightenment.* Urbana: University of Illinois Press, 1971.

Baker, D. W. C. *A Brief History of Texas from Its Earliest Settlement.* New York: A. S. Barnes and Co., 1873.

————, comp. *A Texas Scrapbook. Made Up of the History, Biography, and Miscellany of Texas and Its People.* New York: A. S. Barnes and Co., 1875. Reprint, Austin: Texas State Hsitorical Association, 1991.

Bancroft, Hubert Howe. *Essays and Miscellany.* Vol. 38 of *The Works of Hubert Howe Bancroft.* San Francisco: History Company, 1890.

Bainbridge, John. *The Super-Americans.* Garden City, N.Y.: Doubleday, 1961.

————. *History of the North Mexican States and Texas, 1531–1800.* Vol. 15 of *The Works of Hubert Howe Bancroft.* San Francisco: A. L. Bancroft and Co., 1884.

————. *History of the North Mexican States and Texas, 1801–1889.* Vol. 16 of *The Works of Hubert Howe Bancroft.* San Francisco: History Company, 1889.

————. *Literary Industries.* Vol. 39 of *The Works of Hubert Howe Bancroft.* San Francisco: History Company, 1890.

Barnes, Harry Elmer. *A History of Historical Writing.* 2d ed., rev. New York: Dover Publications, 1963.

Becker, Carl. "Everyman His Own Historian." *American Historical Review* 37 (January 1932): 221–36.

Benedict, H. Y., comp. *A Source Book Relating to the History of the University of Texas: Legislative, Legal, Bibliographical, and Statistical.* Austin: n.p., 1917.

————. "George Pierce Garrison." *Quarterly of the Texas State Historical Association* 14 (January 1911): 173–81.

"Book Reviews and Notices." *Quarterly of the Texas State Historical Association* 8 (July 1904): 87–89.

Bracht, Viktor Frederich. *Texas im Jahre 1848, nach mehrjährigen Beobachtungen dargestellt.* Elberfeld and Iserlohn, Germany: Julius Bäedeker, 1849.

"British Correspondence concerning Texas." *Quarterly of the Texas State Historical Association* 15 (January 1912).

Brown, Frank. "Annals of Travis County and of the City of Austin: From the Earliest Times to the Close of 1875." Typescript. 15 vols. Texas State Library, Archives Division. Austin, n.d.

Brown, John Henry. *History of Texas from 1685 to 1892.* 2 vols. St. Louis: L. E. Daniell, 1892–93.

Buenger, Walter L., and Robert A. Calvert, eds. *Texas through Time: Evolving Interpretations.* College Station: Texas A&M University Press, 1991.

Callcott, George H. *History in the United States, 1800–1860: Its Practice and Purpose.* Baltimore, Md.: Johns Hopkins University Press, 1970.

Caughey, John Walton. *Hubert Howe Bancroft, Historian of the West.* Berkeley and Los Angeles: University of California Press, 1946.

Clark, Harry Hayden, ed. *Transitions in American Literary History.* Durham, N. C.: Duke University Press, 1953.

Clark, L. D. "Texas Historical Writing: A Sample of the Myth at Age 150." *American West* 12 (January/February 1986): 80–81.

Coleman, Robert M. *Houston Displayed; Or, Who Won the Battle of San Jacinto? By a Farmer in the Army.* Velasco, Tex.: n.p., 1837.

Collingwood, R. G. *The Idea of History.* Oxford: Clarendon Press, 1946.

Darby, William. "Province of Texas." *New York Columbian* (3 Aug. 1819). Reprinted in *Niles Weekly Register,* supplement to vol. 16 (7 August 1819): 42–46.

Davis, M. E. M. *Under Six Flags, The Story of Texas.* Boston and London: Ginn and Co., 1897.

DeBow, J. D. B. "Texas—A Province, Republic, and State." *DeBow's Review* 23 (September 1857): 239–67.

Dictionary of American Biography. 20 vols., and 6 supplements to 1980. Published under the auspices of the American Council of Learned Societies. New York: Charles Scribner's Sons, 1928–58.

Dictionary of National Biography. 66 vols. New York: Macmillan, 1885–1901. Reprint, London: Oxford University Press, 1921.

Dunt, Detlef. *Reise nach Texas, nebst Nachrichten von diesem Lande: fuer Deutsche, welche nach Amerika zu gehen beabsichtigen.* Bremen, Germany: Carl Wilh. Wiehe, 1834.

Edward, David Barnett. *The History of Texas; or, The Emigrant's, Farmer's, and Politician's Guide to the Character, Climate, Soil and Productions of that Country: Geographically Arranged and from Personal Observation and Experience.* Cincinnati, Ohio: J. A. James and Co., 1836.

Ehrenberg, Hermann. *Texas Un Seine Revolution.* Leipzig, Germany: Otto Wigand, 1843.

Filisola, Vicente. *Memorias para la Historia de la Guerra de Tejas.* Vol. 1. Mexico City: n.p., 1848. *Memoirs for the History of the War in Texas.* Translated by Wallace Woolsey. Austin: Eakin Press, 1985.

———. *Representación Dirigida al Supremo Gobierno . . . en Defensa de su Honor y Aclaración de sus Operaciones como General en Gefe del Ejercito Sobre Tejas.* Mexico City: Impreso por Ignacio Cumplido, 1836.

Foote, Henry Stuart. *Texas and the Texans; or, The Advance of the Anglo-Americans to the South-west; Including a History of Leading Events in Mexico, from the Conquest by Fernando Cortes to the Termination of the Texas Revolution.* 2 vols. Philadelphia: Thomas Cowperthwaite and Co., 1841.

Frantz, Joe B. "Lone Star Mystique." *American West* 5 (May 1989): 6–9.

Fulmore, Z. T. *The History and Geography of Texas as Told in County Names.* Austin: Steck Co., 1935.

Gambrell, Herbert Pickens. *Mirabeau Buonaparte Lamar, Troubadour and Crusader.* Dallas: Southwest Press, 1934.

Garrison, George Pierce. "Scientific and Literary Historians." *Popular Science Monthly* 58 (November 1900): 92–95.

———. *Texas: A Contest of Civilizations.* New York: Houghton-Mifflin and Co., 1903.

———, ed. *Diplomatic Correspondence of the Republic of Texas.* Pt. 3, vol. 2, pt. 2 of *Annual Report of the American Historical Association for the Year 1908.* Washington, D.C.: U.S. Government Printing Office, 1911.

Geiser, S. W. "Men of Science in Texas, 1820–1880." *Field and Laboratory* 27 (July 1959): 163–256.

Gouge, William M. *The Fiscal History of Texas, Embracing An Account of its Revenues, Debts, and Currency, From the Commencement of the Revolution in 1834 to 1851–52 With Remarks on American Debts.* Philadelphia: Lippincott, Grambo, and Co., 1852.

Gulick, Charles Adams, Jr., and Katherine Elliott, eds. *The Papers of Mirabeau Buonaparte Lamar.* 6 vols. Austin: A. C. Baldwin Printers, 1921–27.

Hartmann, L., and Millard. *Le Texas, ou notice historique sur le Champ d'Asile, comprenant tout ce qui s'est passe depuis la formation jusqu'a la dissolution de cette colonie, les causes qui l'ont, amenee, et la liste de tous les colons Francais, avec des renseignemens utiles à leurs familles, et le plan du champ.* Paris: Chez Beguin, editeur, 1819.

Higham, John. *History, Professional Scholarship in America.* Johns Hopkins Paperback Edition. Baltimore, Md.: Johns Hopkins University Press, 1983.

———. *Writing American History, Essays on Modern Scholarship.* Bloomington: Indiana University Press, 1970.

Historical Magazine 10: (May 1866): 166–67.

"History." *American Quarterly Review* 5 (March 1829): 85–99.

Holley, Mary Austin. *Letters of an Early American Traveller: Mary Austin Holley, Her Life and Her Works.* Edited by Mattie Austin Hatcher. Dallas: Southwest Press, 1933.

———. Mary Austin Holley: The Texas Diary, 1835–1838. Edited by James Perry Bryan. Austin: University of Texas Press, 1965.

———. *Texas.* Lexington, Ky.: J. Clarke and Co., 1836. Reprint, Fred H. and Ella Mae Moore Texas History Reprint Series, Austin: Texas State Historical Association, 1990.

Houston *Telegraph and Texas Register.* 1842.

Houstoun, Mathilda Charlotte (Jesse) Fraser. *Texas and the Gulf of Mexico; Or, Yachting in the New World.* 2 vols. London: John Murray, 1844.

Huntsville *Bench and Bar.* 1857.

Ikin, Arthur. *Texas: Its History, Topography, Agriculture, Commerce, and General Statistics, to Which is Added, a Copy of the Treaty of Commerce Entered into by the Republic of Texas and Great Britain. Designed for the Use of the British Merchant and as a Guide to Emigrants.* London: Sherwood, Gilbert, and Piper, 1841.

James, Will S. *27 Years a Mavrick or Life On a Texas Range.* Chicago: Donahue and Henneberry, 1893.

Jenkins, John H. *Basic Texas Books.* Rev. ed. Austin: Texas State Historical Association, 1988.

———. *Texas History: One Thousand Rare Books, with Additional Sections on Texas Maps, Photographs, and Manuscripts, and a Selection on the Mexican War.* Catalogue 127. Austin: The Jenkins Company, 1980.

Jones, Anson. *Memoranda and Official Correspondence Relating to the Republic of Texas, Its History and Annexation.* 1859. Reprint, Chicago: Rio Grande Press, 1966.

Kammen, Michael. *Mystic Chords of Memory: The Transformation of Tradition in American Culture.* New York: Alfred Knopf, 1991.

———. *Spheres of Liberty: Changing Perceptions of Liberty in American Culture.* Ithaca, N.Y.: Cornell University Press, 1986.

Kendall, George Wilkins. *Narrative of the Texan and Santa Fe Expedition, Comprising a Description of a Tour through Texas and across the Great Southwestern Prairies, the Camanche and Cayuga Hunting-Grounds with an Account of the Sufferings from Want of Food, Losses from Hostile Indians, and Final Capture of the Texans, and Their March, as Prisoners, to the City of Mexico.* New York: Harper and Brothers, 1844.

Kennedy, William. *Texas: The Rise, Progress, and Prospects of the Republic of Texas, in One Volume.* 2d ed. 1841. Reprint, Fort Worth: The Molyneaux Craftsmen, 1925.

Kraus, Michael D., and David D. Joyce. *The Writing of American History.* Rev. ed. Norman: University of Oklahoma Press, 1985.

Lang, Herbert H. "19th Century Historians of the Gulf States." Ph.D. diss., University of Texas at Austin, 1954.

[Lawrence, A. B.] *A History of Texas; or, the Emigrant's Guide to the New Republic, by a Resident Emigrant, Late from the United States.* New York: Nafis and Cornish, 1844.

———. *Texas in 1840, Or the Emigrant's Guide to the New Republic; Being the Result of Observation, Enquiry and Travel in That Beautiful Country, by an Emigrant, Late of the United States.* New York: William W. Allen, 1840.

LeClerc, Frédéric. "Texas and Its Revolution." *Southern Literary Messenger* 7 (May/June, 1841): 398–421.

————. *Texas and Its Revolution.* Translated by James L. Shepherd III. Houston: Anson Jones Press, 1950.

————. *Le Texas et sa revolution.* Paris: H. Fournier et Ce, 1840.

Lee, Rebecca Smith. *Mary Austin Holley, A Biography.* The Elma Dill Russel Spencer Foundation Series, no. 2. Austin: University of Texas Press, 1962.

Lehman-Haupt, Helmut. *The Book in America: A History of the Making and Selling of Books in the United States.* 2d ed. New York: R. R. Bowker Co., 1952.

Levin, David. *History as Romantic Art: Bancroft, Prescott, Motley, and Parkman.* New York: AMS Press, 1967.

Lewis, Richard W. B. *The American Adam: Innocence, Tragedy, and Tradition in the Nineteenth Century.* Chicago: University of Chicago Press, 1955.

"Literary Notices." *Harper's New Monthly Magazine* 14 (January 1857): 265.

Maillard, Nicholas Doran. *The History of the Republic of Texas, from the Discovery of the Country to the Present Time; and the Cause of Her Separation from the Republic of Mexico.* London: Smith, Elder and Co. Cornhill, 1842.

Marten, James. *Texas Divided.* Lexington: University of Kentucky Press, 1990.

Martineau, Harriet. *Society in America.* 2d ed. 2 vols. New York: Saunders and Otley, 1837.

McCaleb, Walter F. Review of *A Comprehensive History of Texas.* Edited by Dudley G. Wooten. *The Dial* 29 (September 1900): 122–24.

McDonald, David R., and Timothy M. Matovina, eds. *Defending Mexican Valor in Texas: José Antonio Navarro's Historical Writings, 1853–1857.* Austin: State House Press, 1995.

McGrath, Sister (Paul of the Cross). *Political Nativism in Texas, 1825–1860.* Washington, D.C.: Catholic University of America, 1930.

McMurtry, Larry. *In a Narrow Grave: Essays on Texas.* Austin: Encino Press, 1968.

McNeill, William H. "Mythistory or Truth, Myth, History, and Historians." *American Historical Review* 91 (February 1986): 1–10.

"The Modern Art and Science of History." *Westminster Review* 30 (October 1842): 337–71.

Moore, Walter, ed. *The Texas Almanac, 1857–1873, A Compendium of Texas History.* Waco: Texian Press, 1967.

Morfi, Juan Agustín. *History of Texas, 1673–1779.* Translated by Carlos Eduardo Castañeda. 2 vols. Albuquerque, N. M.: Quivira Society, 1935. Reprint, New York: Arno Press, 1967.

Morphis, James M. *History of Texas, from Its Discovery and Settlement, with a Description of its Principal Cities and Counties, and the Agricultural, Mineral, and Material Resources of the State.* New York: United States Publishing Co., 1874.

Mott, Frank Luther. *Golden Multitudes: The Story of Best Sellers in the United States.* New York: Macmillan, 1947.

————. *A History of American Magazines, 1741–1850.* Vol. 1. Cambridge: Harvard University Press, 1957.

Nathan, Debbie. "Forget the Alamo." *Texas Monthly,* 26 April 1998, 105, 126–28.

Newell, Chester. *History of the Revolution in Texas, Particularly of the War of 1835 and '36, together with the Latest Geographical, Topographical, and Statistical Accounts of the Country from the Most Authentic Sources.* New York: Wiley and Putnam, 1838. Reprint, The Far Western Frontier Series, New York: Arno Press, 1973.

Niles, John M. *History of South America and Mexico; Comprising Their Discovery, Geography, Politics, Commerce and Revolutions to Which is Annexed, a Geographical and Historical View of Texas, with a Detailed Account of the Texian Revolution and War,* by Hon. L. T. Pease. 2 vols. Hartford, Conn.: H. Huntington, 1844.

Noble, David W. *Historians against History: The Frontier Thesis and the National Covenant in American Historical Writing since 1830*. Minneapolis: University of Minnesota Press, 1965.

O'Gorman, Edmundo. *The Invention of America: An Inquiry into the Historical Nature of the New World and Meaning of Its History*. Bloomington: University of Illinois Press, 1961.

Osterweis, Rollin G. *Romanticism and Nationalism in the Old South*. New Haven, Conn.: Yale University Press, 1949.

Palau y Dulcet, Antonio. *Manuel del Librero Hispano-Americano*. 28 vols. Barcelona and Oxford: Oxford University Press, 1948–77.

Parker, Amos Andrew. *Trip to the West and Texas, Comprising a Journey of Eight Thousand Miles, through New York, Michigan, Illinois, Missouri, Louisiana and Texas, in the Autumn and Winter of 1834–5, Interspersed with Anecdotes, Incidents, and Observations*. Concord: N.H.: White and Fisher, 1835.

Payne, James Sutton. "Texas Historiography in the Twentieth Century: A Study of Eugene C. Barker, Charles W. Ramsdell, and Walter P. Webb." Ph.D. diss., University of Denver, 1972.

Pennybacker, Anna J. Hardwicke. *A History of Texas for Schools*. Rev. ed. Austin: Mrs. Percy V. Pennybacker, 1924.

Pessen, Edward. *Jacksonian America: Society, Personality, and Politics*. Homewood, Ill.: Dorsey Press, 1969.

Pichardo, Fray José Antonio. *Pichardo's Treatise on the Limits of Louisiana and Texas*. Translated and edited by Charles W. Hackett. 4 vols. Austin: University of Texas Press, 1931.

Potter, Reuben Marmaduke. "The Battle of San Jacinto." *Magazine of American History* 4 (1880): 321–50.

———. "The Fall of the Alamo." *Magazine of American History* 2 (January 1878): 1–20.

———. *The Fall of the Alamo: A Reminiscence of the Texas Revolution*. San Antonio: printed on the Herald steam press, 1860.

———. "Texas Admitted to the Union." *Magazine of American History* 10 (August 1883): 100–101.

———. "The Texas Revolution: Distinguished Mexicans Who Took Part in the Revolution of Texas, With Glances At Its Early Events." *Magazine of American History* 2 (October 1878): 577–603.

"A Prophetic Article Published in the *Galveston Civilian* in 1845 [entitled "British & Northern Abolition"]." New York: s.n., 1863.

Raines, C. W. *A Bibliography of Texas*. Austin: Gammel, 1896.

———. Review of *A Comprehensive History of Texas, 1685 to 1897*, by D. G. Wooten. *Quarterly of the Texas State Historical Association* 2 (July 1898): 87–93.

Red, William Stuart, ed. "[W. Y.] Allen's Reminiscences of Texas, 1838–1842." *Southwestern Historical Quarterly* 17 (January 1913): 283–305.

Reid, Samuel Chester, Jr. *The Scouting Expeditions of McCulloch's Texas Rangers . . .* Philadelphia: G. B. Zieber and Co., 1847.

Review of *Lectures on the History of France. North American Review* 75 (July 1852): 247–70.

Review of *The Fiscal History of Texas*, by William M. Gouge. *DeBow's Review* 14 (April 1858): 380–86.

Review of *The History of the Revolution in Texas*, by Rev. Chester Newel [*sic*]. *Dublin Review* 12 (December 1838): 660–67.

Review of *The History of Texas*, by N. D. Maillard. *Monthly Review* 157 (1842): 174–82.

Review of *The History of Texas from Its Earliest Settlement . . .* , by Henderson K. Yoakum. *Putnam's Monthly* 9 (January 1857): 99–100.

Review of *The Life of Napoleon Bounaparte, Emperor of the French,* [by Sir Walter Scott]. *Christian Examiner* 4 (September 1827): 382–430.

Review of *The Rise, Progress, and Prospects of the Republic of Texas,* by William Kennedy. *New York Review* 9 (July 1841): 188–209.

Review of *The Romance of History, England,* by Henry Neele. *Edinburgh Review* 47 (May 1828): 331–67.

Review of *Texas and the Texans . . . ,* [by Henry S. Foote]. *New York Review* 9 (July 1841): 208–209.

Roberts, O. M. "The Proper Work of the Association." *Quarterly of the Texas State Historical Association* 1 (July 1897): 3–8.

Ross, Dorothy. "Historical Consciousness in Nineteenth Century America." *American Historical Review* 89 (October 1984): 909–28.

Smith, Henry Nash. *Virgin Land: The American West as Symbol and Myth.* New York: Vintage Books, 1957. 4th printing, 1962.

Solms-Braunfels, Carl. *Texas, geschildert in Beziehung auf seine geographischen, socialsen, und übrigen Verhaltnisse, mit besonderem Ruecksicht auf die Deutsche Colonisation ein Handbuch fuer Auswanderer nach Texas.* Frankfurt am Main: Johann David Sauerlander's Verlag, 1846.

Sowell, Andrew Jackson. *Rangers and Pioneers of Texas, with a Concise Account of the Early Settlements, Hardships, massacres, Battles, and Wars by Which Texas Was Rescued from the Rule of the Savage and Consecrated to the Empire of Civilization.* San Antonio: Shepard Bros. and Co., 1884.

Stagner, Stephen. "Epics, Science, and the Lost Frontier: Texas Historical Writing, 1836–1936." *Western Historical Quarterly* 12 (April 1981): 165–81.

Stapp, William Preston. *The Prisoners of Perote: Containing a Journal Kept by the Author, Who was Captured by the Mexicans, at Mier, December 25, 1842, and Released from Perote, May 16, 1844.* Philadelphia: G. B. Zieber and Co., 1845.

Stiff, Edward. *A New History of Texas . . . Down to the Present Time: and a History of the Mexican War, including accounts of the Battles of Palo Alto, Resaca de Palma, and the Taking of Monterrey.* Cincinnati, Ohio: G. Conclin, 1847.

———. *The Texan Emigrant: Being a Narration of the Adventure of the Author in Texas, and a Description of the Soil, Climate, Productions, Minerals, Towns, Bays, Harbors, Rivers, Institutions, and Manners and Customs of the Inhabitants of That Country; Together with the Principal Incidents of Fifteen Years Revolution in Mexico: and Embracing A Condensed Statement of Interesting Events in Texas, from the First European Settlement in 1692, down to the Year 1840.* Cincinnati, Ohio: George Conclin, 1840. Reprint, Waco: Texian Press, 1968.

Streeter, Thomas W. *Bibliography of Texas, 1795–1845.* 5 vols. Cambridge: Harvard University Press, 1955–60.

Tatum, Bowen C., Jr. "A Texas Patriot." *Texas Bar Journal* 53 (September 1970): 722.

Tebbel, John William. *A History of Book Publishing in the United States.* Vol. 1. New York: R. R. Bowker Co., 1972.

The Texas Almanac for 1857, with Statistics, Historical and Biographical Sketches &c., Relating to Texas. Galveston: Richardson and Co., 1856.

Thoreau, Henry David. *Works of Henry David Thoreau.* Edited by Lily Owens. New York: Avenel Books, 1981.

Thorpe, Thomas Bangs. *Our Army on the Río Grand, Being a Short Account of the Important Events Transpiring from the Time of the Removal of the "Army of Occupation," from Corpus Christi, to the Surrender of Matamoros . . .* Philadelphia: Carey and Hart, 1846.

Thrall, Homer S. *A Brief History of Methodism in Texas.* Nashville, Tenn.: M. E. Church, South, 1889.

————. *A History of Texas, from the Earliest Settlements to the Year 1885, with an Appendix Containing the Constitution of the State of Texas, Adopted November, 1875, and the Amendments of 1883. For Use in Schools and for General Readers.* New York: University Publishing Co., 1876. Rev. ed., 1885, 1892.

————. *The People's Illustrated Almanac, Texas Hand-book and Immigrants' Guide, for 1880, Being an Index to Texas, Her People, Laws, State and Local Governments, Schools, Churches, Railroads, and Other Improvements and Institutions . . . with Chronological History of the State for 1879.* St. Louis: N. D. Thompson and Co., 1880.

————. *A Pictorial History of Texas from the Earliest Visits of European Adventurers, to A.D. 1879.* St. Louis: N. D. Thompson and Co., 1879.

Tocqueville, Alexis de. *Democracy in America.* Edited by J. P. Mayer and translated by George Lawrence. Perennial Library. New York: Harper and Row, 1988.

Trollope, Frances. *Domestic Manners of the Americans.* 3d ed. 2 vols. London: Whitaker, Treacher and Co., Gilbert and Rivington, printers, 1832.

Tyler, Ron, Douglas E. Barnett, Roy R. Barkely, Penelope C. Anderson, and Mark K. Odnitz, eds. *The New Handbook of Texas.* 6 vols. Austin: Texas State Historical Association, 1996.

Van Tassel, David D. "From Learned Society to Professional Organization: The American Historical Association, 1884–1900." *American Historical Review* 89 (October 1984): 929–56.

————. *Recording America's Past; An Interpretation of the Development of Historical Studies in America, 1607–1884.* Chicago: University of Chicago Press, 1960.

Van West, Carroll. "Democratic Ideology and the Antebellum Historian: The Case of Henderson Yoakum." *Journal of the Early Republic* 3 (fall 1983): 319–39.

A Visit to Texas, Being the Journal of a Traveller Through Those Parts Most Interesting to American Settlers, with Descriptions of the Scenery, &c., &c. New York: Goodrich and Wiley, 1834.

West, Elizabeth Howard. "A Translation of Bonilla's Report," *Quarterly of the Texas State Historical Association* 8 (July 1904): 3–78.

Wharton, Clarence R. *History of Fort Bend County.* San Antonio: The Naylor Co., 1939.

Whitaker, Arthur P., ed. *Latin America and the Enlightenment.* 2d ed. Ithaca, N.Y.: Cornell University Press, 1961.

Wilbarger, John Wesley. *Indian Depredations in Texas: Reliable Accounts of Battles, Wars, Adventures, Forays, Murders, Massacres, Etc., Etc., Together with Biographical Sketches of Many of the Most Noted Indian Fighters and Frontiersmen of Texas.* Austin: Hutchings Printing House, 1889.

Williams, Amelia W., and Eugene C. Barker, eds. *The Writings of Sam Houston, 1813–1863.* 8 vols. Austin: University of Texas Press, 1939.

Woodward, C. Vann. *Thinking Back: The Perils of Writing History.* Baton Rouge: Louisiana State University Press, 1986.

Wooten, Dudley G. *A Complete History of Texas for Schools, Colleges, and General Use.* Dallas: Texas History Co., 1899.

———, ed. *A Comprehensive History of Texas, 1685 to 1897*. 2 vols. Dallas: William G. Scarff, 1898. Reprint, Austin: Texas State Historical Association, 1986.

Yoakum, Henderson [King]. *History of Texas from Its First Settlement in 1865 to Its Annexation to the United States in 1846*. 2 vols. New York: Redfield, 1855. Reprint, Austin: Steck Co., 1935.

Yoakum, Thomas P. "Henderson Yoakum, Texas Historian." *Frontier Times* 27 (July 1950): 288–92.

NEWSPAPERS

Dallas Daily Herald. 1874–1875.
Dallas Morning News. 1945.
Dallas Times Herald. 1945.
Dallas Weekly Herald. 1874–1875.
Galveston Civilian. 1845.

Index

ISBN 1-58544-314-X